World Population
and
Human Values

Also by Jonas Salk

Man Unfolding
The Survival of the Wisest

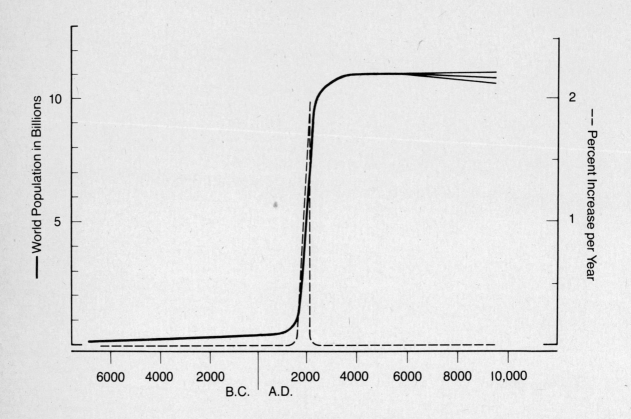

World Population and Human Values

A New Reality

JONAS SALK
and
JONATHAN SALK

1817

HARPER & ROW, PUBLISHERS, NEW YORK

Cambridge, Philadelphia, San Francisco, London, Mexico City, São Paulo, Sydney

FIRST EDITION

Designer: Sue Crooks

Library of Congress Cataloging in Publication Data
Salk, Jonas, 1914–
    World population and human values.
    Bibliography: p.
    1. Population. 2. Population—History. 3. Social problems. 4. Human ecology. 5. Values. I. Salk, Jonathan. II. Title.
HB871.S17   1981   304.6   79–1683
                         AACR2
ISBN 0–06–013778–9
ISBN 0–06–090907–2 (pbk.)

81 82 83 84 85 10 9 8 7 6 5 4 3 2 1
81 82 83 84 85 10 9 8 7 6 5 4 3 2 1

To Mark Frank—
who asked

Contents

Preface

This book originated in a request my father received for a commentary, from his point of view as a biomedical scientist and author, on United Nations assessments and projections of world population trends. He assembled a graphic summary of the data and added material based on his earlier book, *The Survival of the Wisest.** The result was a brief report in the form of a pictographic essay. A copy of that report was submitted to Harper & Row, who expressed an interest in publishing it as a book.

I first became involved in the project when he asked for my comments. When I told him of my reactions he encouraged me to try my hand at strengthening the report with the intent of making it into a book. In my first efforts, I completely reworked and restructured the original manuscript. The length and tone of the version I produced, however, did not fit with the original concept of a short, graphic piece intended to be used to convey information quickly and effectively. Over a period of many months, we reconciled these different approaches in a way that retains the best elements of both styles.

Our collaboration is one example of the process of divergence, convergence, and reconciliation discussed in this essay. We, two people from different eras, parent and child with much in common, yet also with different points of view and aesthetics, have worked together toward a common goal. It is our hope that this has resulted in a book more useful to the reader than either of us would have produced alone.

JONATHAN D. SALK

* Jonas Salk. New York: Harper & Row, 1973.

Acknowledgments

We would like to acknowledge the very valuable assistance of MaryEllen Diefenbach in the early stages of this work and the patient, competent, and supportive help of Barbara L. Robinson in the assembly of the graphs and text.

Thanks are due to the United Nations Fund for Population Activities (UNFPA) for its generous support and to the United Nations for allowing us the use of its libraries. We want also to thank Rafael Salas, Tarzie Vittachi, and T. N. Krishnan of the UNFPA—Dr. Salas for his confidence and affirmation, Tarzie for moral support, suggestions, and encouragement throughout, and Dr. Krishnan for providing valuable suggestions about the presentation of several key ideas. Shunichi Inoue, Chief of the Estimates and Projections Division of the United Nations, kindly supplied unpublished data on long-range projections. Carl Haub of the Population Reference Bureau made a number of suggestions on our discussion of the demographic material, and though he should not be held responsible for our final presentation, we are very grateful for his comments.

We also acknowledge the invaluable contributions of many friends and colleagues who read and commented on the manuscript in its final stages.

Of the many at Harper & Row who patiently made our manuscript into a book, we would like to thank those with whom we have had personal contact: Cass Canfield, Jr., Lydia Link, William Monroe, Pamela Jelley, and, especially, Frank Ronan, who painstakingly prepared the graphics to our specifications.

Personally, our deepest thanks must go to the following who, at various times provided advice, intellectual challenge, moral support, and meals: Françoise Gilot, Elizabeth Moore, N. Jamás, and Peter, Darrell, and Donna Salk.

Note

Preparation of the report upon which this book is based was made possible by a grant from the United Nations Fund for Population Activities of the United Nations Secretariat.

Introduction

Collectively and individually, we are at a critical time in human history and human evolution. The crisis is evident both in the commentary of contemporary writers and thinkers and in the personal experience of people throughout the world. It is apparent in the rate of population growth, in exploitation of natural resources, and in the widespread occurrence of social and political disturbances. Nations and individuals are experiencing an increase in internal and external tensions and conflicts. Conversely, there is a growing awareness of trends toward greater understanding and cooperation, toward peaceful rather than war-like resolution of conflicts, and toward a deeper awareness of the subtleties of physical, biological, and human nature.

In this brief volume we offer a perspective to provide understanding of the perplexing nature of our time. Through a discussion of world population trends and changing human values, three ideas will emerge: one, that although disaster threatens, its avoidance is possible; two, that we possess the capacity to meet our present problems and to resolve them humanely; and three, that changes have already become evident, both in world population growth and in human values, that point toward a positive outcome of this crisis.

We have focused on world population for a number of reasons. First, the request for a report on which this book is based came from the United Nations Fund for Population Activities (UNFPA), which asked for a commentary on United Nations projections of population growth. Second, the rapidly increasing world population is a basic and powerful force in the world today and it is important that we be aware of long-range trends and understand the forces underlying population's explosive growth. Third, demographic data provide a basis on which to discuss the relationship between changes in population growth patterns and changes in human attitudes, values, and behavior.

Even though they are but part of a larger complex of social, political, economic, and cultural factors, we have focused on value changes. A great deal of attention has been given to the forms of large social structures, and they are, of course, important. However, cruelty, exploitation, and repression, as well as humane behavior, mutual collaboration, and freedom, have all existed in a variety of social and political settings. It is our intent to focus primarily on change and evolution of fundamental values and attitudes.

The basic image used in this essay is the sigmoid growth curve. It represents a general pattern of change that is seen in many physical and biological systems: a pattern of progressive acceleration changing to progressive deceleration, culminating in dynamic equilibrium at a steady-state plateau. Though we focus on the recent acceleration of population growth, similar trends have been apparent in consumption of energy, in rate of growth of scientific knowledge, and, as many people feel subjectively, in the rapidity of change in personal and social life. In this discussion, we apply the image to population and then to changing human attitudes, values, and behavior; however, some readers will undoubtedly see ways in which this curve is applicable to other areas of change in human relationships and experience.

Many books and essays have appeared in recent years that describe from other points of view the same phenomenon of epochal transformation. Although our focus is on world population and human values, this work is conceptually related to others that have focused on energy, technology, economics, and politics. The perspective offered in this essay is, we believe, complementary to and a natural extension of these.

This is a personal essay; we are not scholars in demography or in human behavior. We have attempted to present the population picture accurately and to interpret the data responsibly. In the course of the essay, we have necessarily touched on knowledge and ideas that fall in the areas of evolutionary theory, sociology, anthropology, political science, economics, ecology, as well as demography. Since we are not specialists in all these areas, we may occasionally have made statements that will be considered overly simplified to those more knowledgeable. If we have, we apologize in advance and hope that we have not misled the reader nor have obscured the main ideas of the essay.

The reader may note a paucity of specific, topical examples. The first reason for this is that, in order to keep the book light and brief, it was undesirable to include extensive discussion of specific issues. A further reason is that specific references to current issues tend to trigger a chain of associations and emotions in the reader that might obscure the point intended. Since our purpose is to look at underlying processes, we have deliberately tried to avoid evoking such responses by being judicious and sparing in the choice of examples.

The form of the book is different from most. It is a "pictographic essay"—a kind of slide presentation contained within the pages of a book. Although we sometimes found this form constraining in the preparation of text, it has, on the whole, allowed for a clear presentation of the population data, which forms a major part of this book, and of the discussion of changing human values, which requires the visual image of the sigmoid curve. Through a series of pictures, supplemented with text, information is made available to those not ordinarily exposed to the data and ideas presented here.

The book is divided into five parts. Part I introduces the sigmoid curve. In Part II, demographic data are presented revealing the emergence of an epochal change and a new reality of world population trends. In Part III, we introduce the concept of two distinct epochs in history—a time of progressive acceleration of growth, and a time of progressive deceleration—and we discuss expected differences in human values between the two periods of time. In Part IV, we consider some of the conflicts and paradoxes inherent in the change of values, and in Part V, we discuss the convergence and reconciliation of divergent trends that can be anticipated to occur in the decades to come. In order to maintain the flow of the presentation, citation of sources for the population data and for relevant textual material are omitted from the body of the book and are contained in a separate section.

Few can meaningfully interpret the past, and no one can reliably predict the future. In this short essay, we provide a long-range perspective, including past and future, that we hope will be helpful in comprehending the forces and trends that underlie the present period of crisis. If we are able to provide, for

xvii

some, a deeper understanding of the present and some glimpse of the future, our purpose will have been served. If, in addition, we provide reinforcement for those who feel, in spite of indications to the contrary, that there is, within the nature of human beings and within the human mind, the capacity for responding to present crises with the creation of a healthier, more humane, and more satisfying future, our deeper hopes will have been fulfilled.

PART I

Sigmoid Curves

In this essay, the sigmoid curve will be used as a "thinking tool" and as a symbol. Its shape reflects a law of nature that governs growth in living systems, and reflects the transformational character of change in our time.

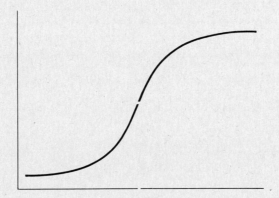

In this figure, and in those that follow, the horizontal axis represents time and the vertical axis represents number. In the first, upturned portion of the curve, population growth follows a pattern of acceleration; in the second part, growth decelerates and a plateau is reached. The gap in the curve emphasizes the point of inflection—the point of change from accelerating growth to decelerating growth.

In Part I, through examples of animal and yeast populations, we will introduce this curve.

From the beginning of the Christian era, the size of the human population grew gradually for about 16 centuries and then with increasing speed through the nineteenth century. This gradual but progressive acceleration was followed by a sudden steep rise in the twentieth century—a consequence of the scientific-technologic-industrial revolution, which has had the effect of making it possible to sustain a human population far larger than ever before.

FIGURE 1

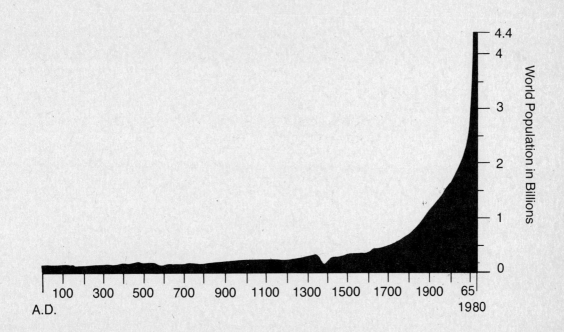

The sharp increase in the size of human population in recent times, as seen on the preceding page, has raised the reasonable question, "Will the curve continue to rise at its present rate, will it crash, or will it bend and assume a sigmoid shape?" The question and the alternative answers are implicit in this picture.

FIGURE 2

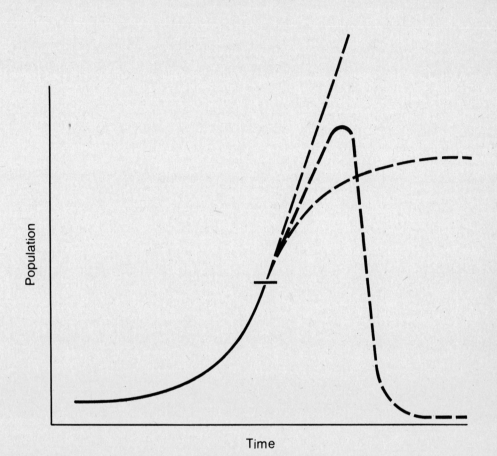

If the curve will inflect, when might this occur and at what level will population size plateau?

That an inflection can be anticipated is suggested by the figures in the pages to follow. Later, in Part II, evidence will be presented to indicate that the inflection of the human population growth curve is beginning; however, the level of the plateau of this curve is still uncertain and will be subject to human influence.

FIGURE 3

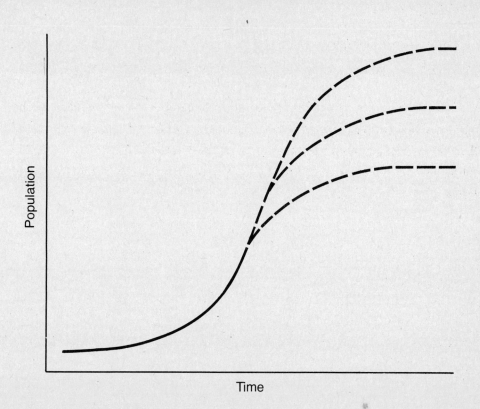

The S-shaped growth curve is seen in many living systems. A few examples will be presented before focusing on human population growth.

This figure is a plot of the growth of a population of fruit flies in a laboratory experiment. A small number of flies were introduced into a chamber of fixed size and the increase in population was observed over a period of approximately five weeks. The population grew slowly at first and then more rapidly as the numbers of flies increased. After about two and a half weeks, however, growth rates began to slow. Over the next two and a half weeks, the number of flies being born approached the number dying, and the curve reached a plateau of approximately 200 flies.

FIGURE 4

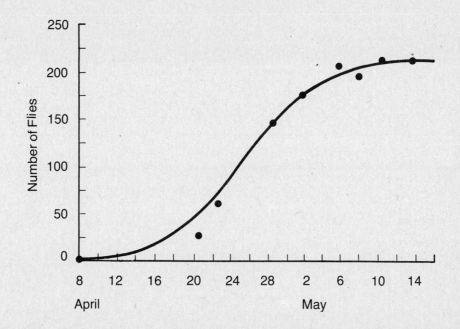

The sigmoid pattern is also observed in the growth of a population of microorganisms. This figure indicates that a population of yeast cells, over a period of 18 hours, follows a similar pattern of increase followed by decrease in growth rate, and attainment of a plateau.

This and the preceding figure indicate that under the conditions of these two studies, population growth slows and reaches a plateau. Figure 6 indicates what happens when conditions are changed.

FIGURE 5

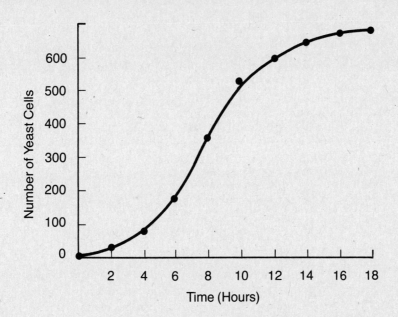

The effect of external influences on growth is shown here in observations made of yeast cultures maintained over periods extending up to 120 hours. The growth curve of the control culture (shown at the top) reveals a sigmoid pattern.

By neutralizing the acid produced in the course of growth—a process that has the effect of ameliorating the negative effects of waste products in the environment (a process equivalent to improved sanitation)—a noticeably higher plateau was reached, as seen in the second curve.

The three other curves show the effect of increase in food supply and removing waste products by changing the culture medium every 24 hours, every 12 hours, or every 3 hours. To sustain population growth at these levels would require an uninterrupted input of food and the simultaneous elimination of the waste products of metabolism. Failure of either would result in a catastrophic collapse in population size.

FIGURE 6

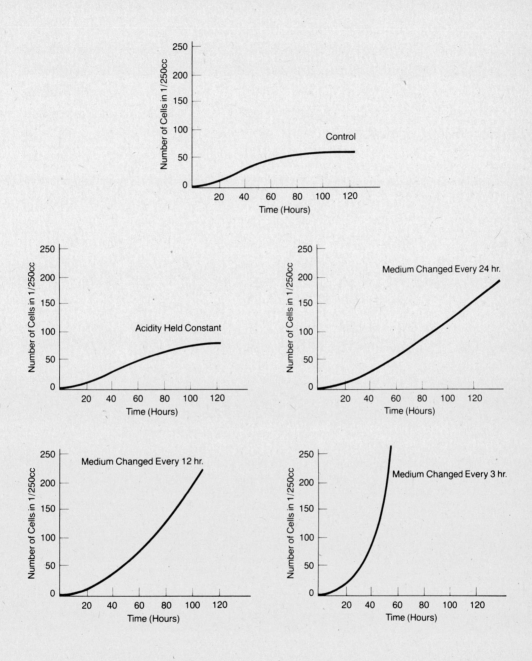

In this study of a population of sheep, we see that after a period of exponential growth, a plateau was reached approximately 30 years after introduction of animals into an area of limited size and that this plateau continued for at least 70 years, the full period of observation.

Each of the preceding sigmoid curves exhibits different rates of change, some counted in minutes, some in hours, some in days, months, or years. Various populations react in different time frames depending on the nature of the organism and on the conditions in which they live.

FIGURE 7

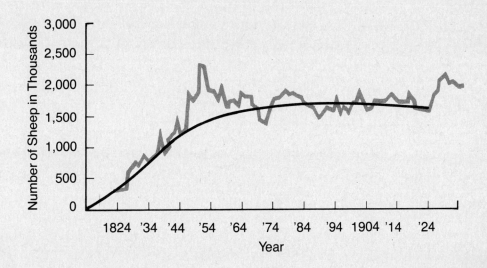

In nature different species have evolved different strategies for survival. In some species, populations fluctuate in size according to a species-specific rhythm. In others, large numbers of individuals are produced in short periods of time under temporarily favorable conditions. In still others, population size remains relatively stable.

The brown lemming, as seen in this figure, is reputed to go through cyclic periods of very rapid population increase followed by a precipitous decline.

In evolution, human beings are among those species adapted to relative stability of population size, and human population groups have not exhibited this kind of extreme, regular fluctuation. It is unlikely that the human species will follow a similar pattern unless large numbers are periodically decimated by famine and/or nuclear holocaust.

FIGURE 8

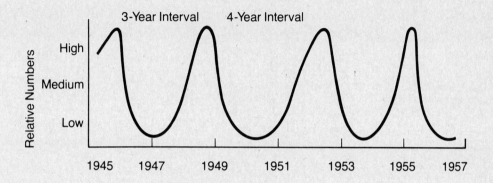

19

The curve presented on the opposite page suggests that human population size will increase indefinitely. As indicated in the preceding charts, however, the curve can be expected to inflect and either plateau or descend sharply. When might this occur?

In the graphs and tables in the following section, we will see that, in many parts of the world and in the world as a whole, population growth is beginning to slow and a plateau is projected.

FIGURE 9

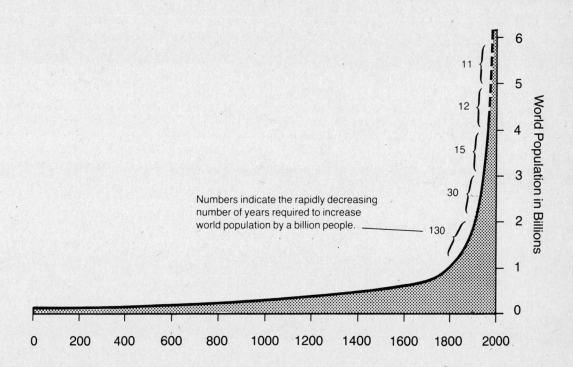

Numbers indicate the rapidly decreasing
number of years required to increase
world population by a billion people. ———— 130

World Population in Billions

SUMMARY

In Part I, through examples of growth of populations in closed systems, the sigmoid curve was introduced.

After a period of slow growth, human population size has increased sharply in recent centuries. Except for the sun as a constant source of energy, the earth can be seen as a closed system and, by inference from the examples given, we can expect the human population growth curve to follow a sigmoid pattern. The level of the plateau is still uncertain, however, and is subject to human influence.

In the years to come, we face the challenge of understanding and facilitating a slowing of human population growth and, ultimately, of adapting to the conditions associated with a relatively constant population size.

PART II

World Population Trends

For thousands of years before agriculture, human population increased very slowly. In response to environmental adversity and population pressures, agriculture emerged, making more food and energy available to support greater numbers of human beings. A pattern of gradual increase thus continued throughout the agricultural period. In the last several centuries, scientific, technologic, and industrial developments have further raised the carrying capacity of the planet, contributing to the recent sharp rise in population.

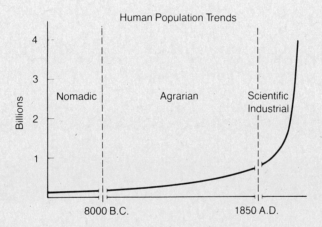

The factors involved in human population growth are far more complex than those affecting the populations seen in Part I. The picture is immensely complicated by sociocultural factors and by technology, which has made new forms of energy available. Marked differences between patterns of population growth in the technologically more and less developed regions of the world are also a factor. In this section we will present some aspects of human population trends and present projections that indicate an anticipated plateau in human population size.

In this figure we see again that human population increased slowly throughout pre- and early history. A dip in the fourteenth century was the result of widespread epidemics of bubonic plague. In a few generations, however, the population returned to the previous level and then resumed its pattern of gradual but progressive growth. In the seventeenth, eighteenth, and nineteenth centuries the development of technology and new sources of energy raised the carrying capacity of the planet to a level far higher than ever before. The development of means for the control of infectious and nutritional deficiency diseases as well as improvements in sanitation and nutrition reduced mortality and had the effect of increasing rates of growth and increasing population size and density. The effects of these developments are analogous to those induced by frequently changing the culture medium in the yeast cultures in Figure 6. The persistent increase in growth rate has continued into the twentieth century, culminating in the explosive growth in population size that has become apparent in recent decades.

FIGURE 10

World Population Growth Through History

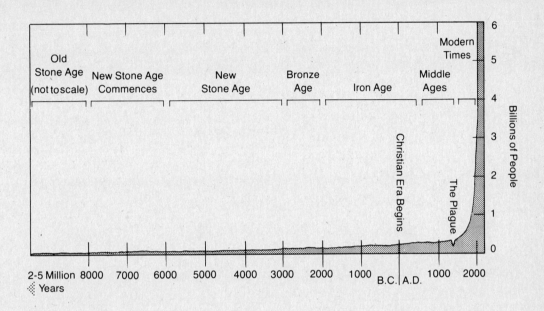

This graph shows the growth of the human population estimated over the period 1650 to 1980. In the hundred years between 1825 and 1925, world population size grew from approximately one billion to nearly two billion, and then nearly doubled again in the next 50 years, going from two to four billion. The second half of the most recent doubling occurred in less than 15 years.

FIGURE 11

Estimated World Population, 1650–1980

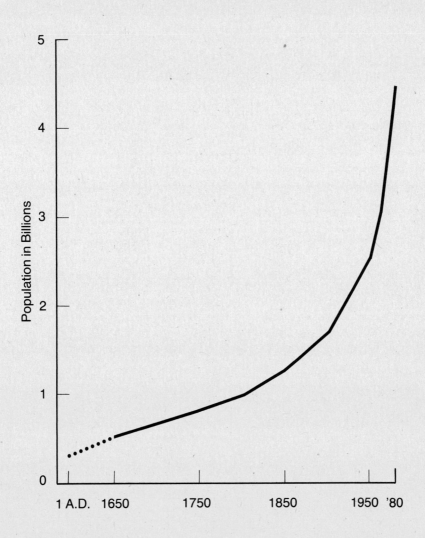

World population size is shown here for the period from 1950–1978 with projections to the year 2000. The three lines after 1978 represent high, medium, and low projections.

Population projections are based on present knowledge of continually changing trends. As such, they cannot be taken as firm predictions of the future, but, in the following figures, they do provide us with a useful perspective for viewing and understanding the present human situation.

FIGURE 12

World Population, 1950–2000
(high, medium, and low variants)

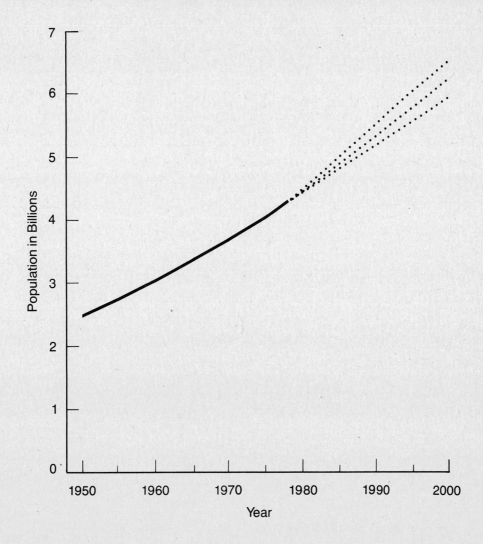

The differences in size of the more and less developed regions of the world are shown here for the period 1950–1975, with high, medium, and low estimated projections to the year 2000.

The more and less developed regions are grouped as follows:

More Developed

Northern America	Japan
All regions of Europe	Australia
U.S.S.R	New Zealand

Less Developed

All regions of Africa	All regions of Asia
South America	(except Japan)
Middle America	Melanesia, Micronesia,
Caribbean	Polynesia

Population is growing faster in the less developed regions and, as a result, the difference between the two regions is expected to increase at least through the end of the century.

On a world scale, human population in 1950 was 2.5 billion, in 1980 over 4 billion, and by the year 2000 it is estimated to reach approximately 6 billion. At that point, 80 percent of the world population will be inhabitants of what are now the less developed countries.

FIGURE 13

Population of More and Less Developed Regions, 1950–2000
(high, medium, and low variants)

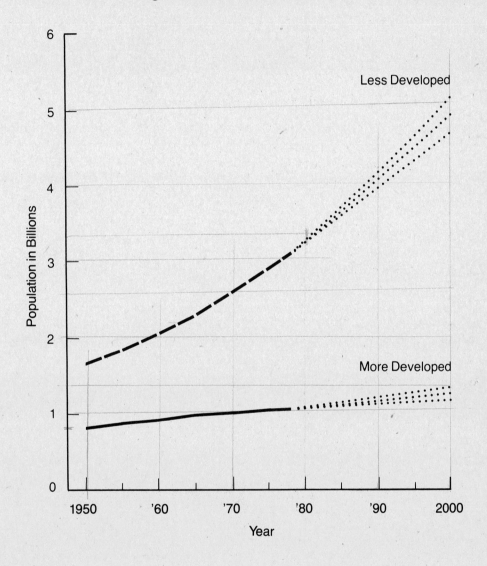

Here the *rates of growth*, expressed as percent annual increase in population in the more and less developed regions, are shown over the period 1950–2000.

According to these projections, the growth rates in the developing countries reached a maximum level of approximately 2.4 percent per year in the decade 1960–1970 and are expected to decrease thereafter. The decline will not be fully evident until 1980–1985, after which it is expected to fall below 2 percent per annum by 1990–1995. In the more developed countries, a more modest peak of approximately 1.3 percent per year was reached around 1950, and growth rates in these areas are expected to decline to a level of 0.5 percent by the year 2000.

FIGURE 14

Rates of Growth
(medium variant)

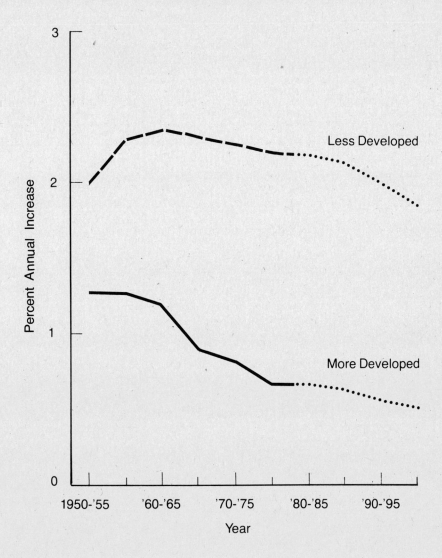

Growth rates and population doubling times° for selected countries in both the more and less developed regions are shown here. It is clear that growth rates are slower and doubling time is longer in the more developed regions.

It is noteworthy that, in a few Western European nations, growth rates have fallen below replacement levels in recent years. This has been cause for some concern and has prompted governments to encourage higher birth rates.

° Population doubling time is the time it would take the present population to double if growth rates were to remain constant at the present level.

FIGURE 15

Growth Rates and Population Doubling Times for Selected Countries
in More and Less Developed Regions

Country	Growth Rates Percent annual increase (1975-1980)	Doubling Time (years)
LESS DEVELOPED		
Kenya	3.9	18
Nigeria	3.2	22
Egypt	3.0	23
Mexico	2.5	28
Brazil	2.4	29
India	2.1	33
China	1.2	58
MORE DEVELOPED		
U.S.S.R.	0.8	86
U.S.A.	0.8	95
France	0.4	178
U.K.	0.1	693
Sweden	0.1	1155
Austria	-0.1	>>
W. Germany	-0.2	>>

A comparison of crude birth and death rates in the less and more developed regions reveals that both are higher in the former. The degree of difference between the two rates is substantially greater in the less developed regions, accounting for the disproportionately high rate of population increase in these areas, as seen in Figures 14 and 15.

In the developing countries, death rates fell faster than birth rates prior to 1970–1975, resulting in increase in growth rates. After this period, death rates are expected to begin to level while birth rates will continue to fall, resulting in a decrease in growth rates. In the more developed regions, on the other hand, death rates have remained essentially constant since 1950 while birth rates have continued, gradually, to approach mortality. These relative changes in birth and death rates account for the changes in rates of growth seen in the two regions (Figure 14).

The reasons for the decline in birth rates (and the associated drop in growth rates) are complex and not completely understood, but it appears that, as socio-economic, educational, and health conditions (including life expectancy at birth) of traditional societies improve, it becomes economically advantageous for families to have fewer children. This change occurred earlier in the more developed regions and is now beginning to occur in the developing areas (see Notes).

FIGURE 16

Crude Birth and Death Rates
(high, medium, and low variants)

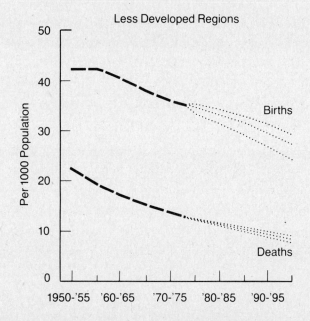

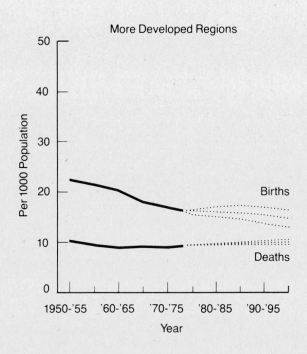

An essential factor in the decline in birth rates seen in many parts of the world is the availability of birth control and family planning programs. This is, however, only part of a more complex set of influences.

The four graphs on the opposite page depict the relationship between birth rates and four other variables—infant mortality, use of health care, age at marriage, and the female literacy rate—in Sri Lanka. A causal relationship among these variables has not been established, and we do not intend to claim such a relationship here. Also, conditions vary from country to country, and this example may not apply everywhere. Nevertheless, it can be seen that, over a period of 50 years, birth rates in Sri Lanka have declined as infant mortality has decreased and as health care availability, age at marriage, and the female literacy rate increased.

It has long been assumed that a fall in birth rates in developing countries comes only with modernization and industrial development. Data like these, obtained from a few developing areas, suggest that increase in the availability of education and health services play a role of great importance in the decline of birth rates, even in areas that have not reached a high level of economic and industrial development (see Notes).

FIGURE 17

Social Factors and Fertility in Sri Lanka

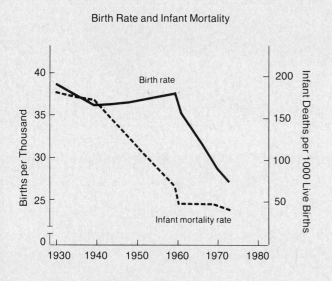

Birth Rate and Infant Mortality

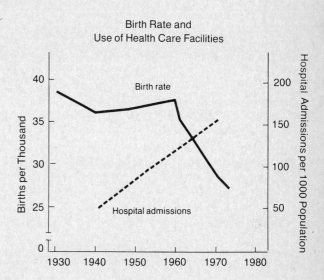

Birth Rate and
Use of Health Care Facilities

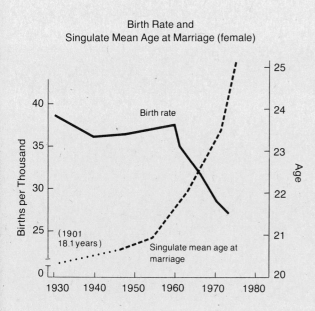

Birth Rate and
Singulate Mean Age at Marriage (female)

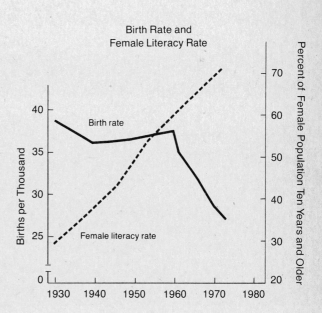

Birth Rate and
Female Literacy Rate

43

If curves such as those in Figure 16 are extended into the past, some of the origins of the present disparity between growth rates in the more and less developed regions are apparent.

In the more developed areas, death rates began to fall perceptibly in the 1800s, while birth rates remained relatively constant. This resulted in an increase of population. After a lag period, however, birth rates also began to fall but still remained higher than death rates.

In the less developed countries, the fall in death rates occurred in response to assistance in public health and nutrition. Hence, the decline in mortality rates occurred later and was sharper than in the more developed regions. This resulted in very rapid increase in population. In the less developed regions, a decline in birth rates has just begun and is expected to continue.

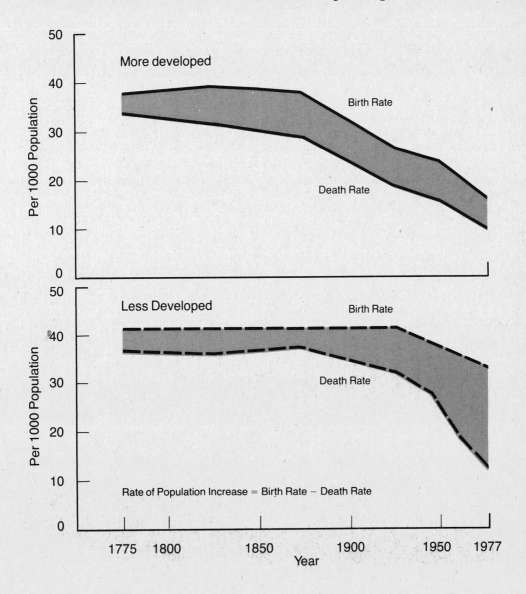

FIGURE/18

Birth and Death Rates: More and Less Developed Regions, 1775–1977

45

The two charts at the right show the age distribution in the populations of the more and less developed regions as of 1975. Population size will continue to increase in the less developed areas even after birth rates fall to replacement levels.* The increase in population will come as the large proportion of young people at the base of the right-hand pyramid move into the medium age group and have children of their own. After the point at which birth rates reach replacement levels, population size will continue to increase, often for as long as a century.

* When birth rates are equal to death rates, they are said to be at replacement levels.

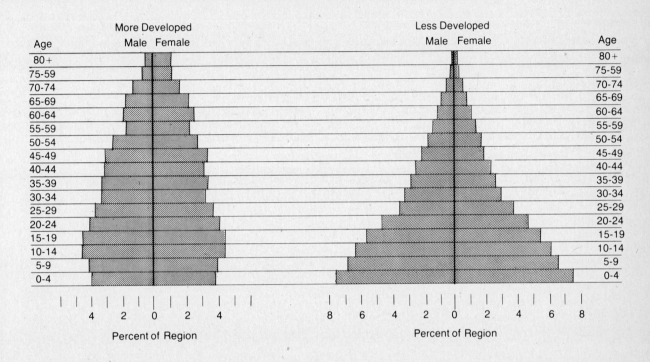

FIGURE 19

Population Distribution by Age and Sex, 1975
(medium variant)

As indicated in the preceding figure, the median age has been uniformly lower in the less developed countries. Although the median age in both regions is rising, the difference between the two will continue for some time to come.

FIGURE 20

Median Ages
(medium variant)

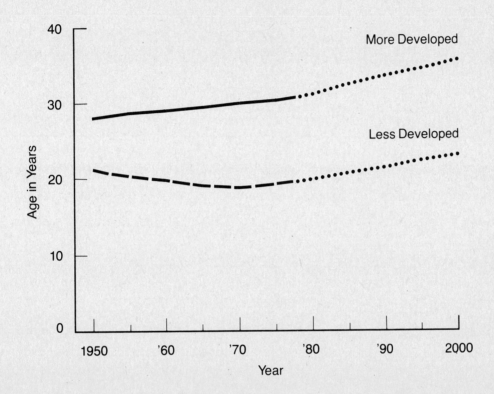

Life expectancy in the less developed regions is rising steeply, but it continues to be much lower than in the more developed regions. Average life expectancy in the less developed regions in the year 2000 will still be below the level attained in the more developed countries in the year 1950, although significant gains in this respect may have been made and the difference will be much reduced.

FIGURE 21

Life Expectancy
(high, medium, and low variants)

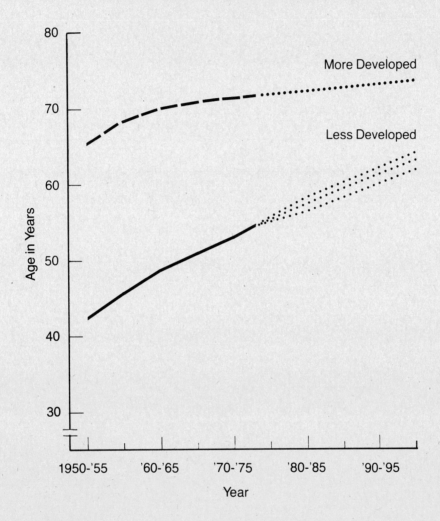

An interesting difference in sex ratios exists between the more and less developed regions of the world, a difference that shows a gradual tendency toward narrowing. There are more men than women in the less developed regions, and more women than men in the more developed world.

In the less developed regions, this ratio is partially a result of higher death rates for women. The higher death rate is the result of the greater risk associated with pregnancy and the burden of bearing a large number of children in a lifetime. Another factor may be the preferential attitude toward male babies that has existed in some traditional societies. When male children are preferred, they receive better care and therefore have better chances of surviving than female children. Another major factor is that the higher proportion of males that exists at birth in all human populations (105-106 males per 100 females) is more apparent in the predominantly younger populations of the less developed countries.

A higher ratio of females to males is evident in the more developed countries where women live longer than men. This ratio is also, in part, a reflection of loss of men in the recent world wars, the effect of which is diminishing.

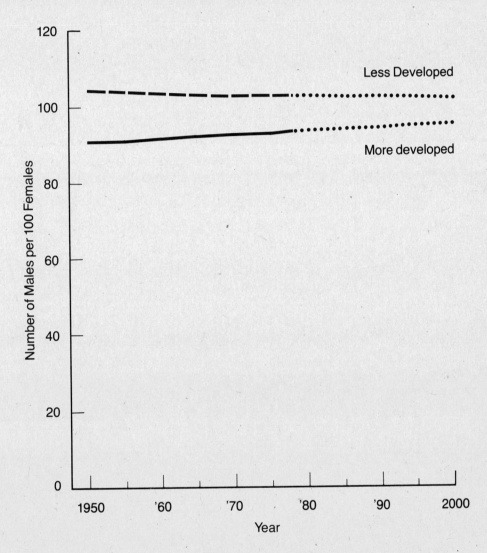

FIGURE 22

Sex Ratios
(medium variant)

Child/woman ratios are also markedly different in the more and less developed regions. In the less developed areas, there are presently about twice the number of children under five years old for each woman than there are in the more developed countries. This suggests that, in the less developed areas, women's lives tend to be more heavily involved with childbearing and childrearing than in the industrialized regions. The disparity in child/woman ratios is expected to narrow by the end of the century as a result of the continued fall in birth rates in the developing areas.

FIGURE 23

Child/Woman Ratios
(medium variant)

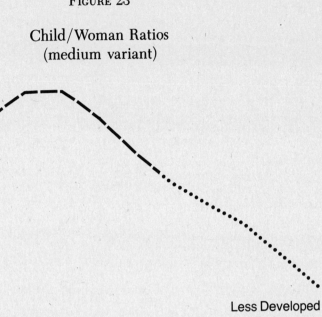

55

A comparison of age distributions also reveals, in the less developed regions, a significantly higher proportion of individuals under age 15. Because many in the age groups under 15 and over 64 are less productive, economically, than those between 15 and 64, the proportions of older and younger to the medium age group are often called "dependency ratios."

Dependency ratios are lower and relatively constant in the developed regions, reflecting the evenness and stability of the age structure of those populations. The dependency ratios are expected to decline in the less developed regions as (a) the population under age 15 declines with fall in birth rates, and (b) as the presently large numbers of young begin to move into the intermediate age group.

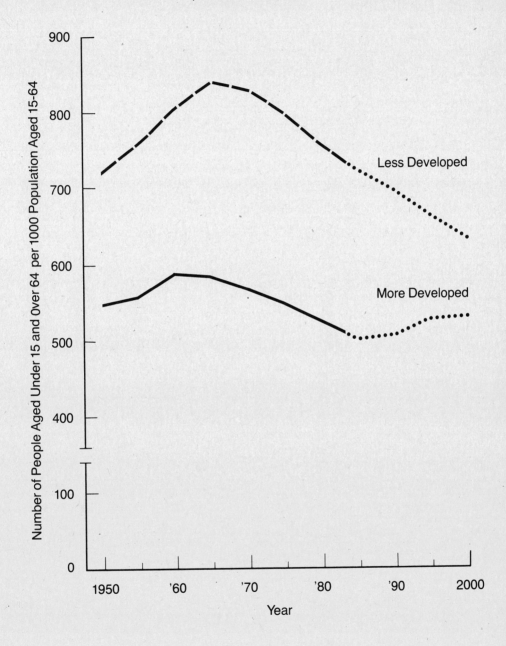

FIGURE 24

Dependency Ratios
(medium variant)

The proportion of the population living in urban areas is rising both in the more and the less developed areas of the world. However, there is a wide difference between the two that will continue for some time. While it is estimated that the proportion of people living in an urban setting in the more developed countries will have increased from about 53 percent in 1950 to 79 percent by the year 2000, the corresponding levels for the developing countries are approximately 17 percent and 44 percent, respectively. By the year 2000, half of the world population will be living in cities and towns.

Figure 25

Proportion of Urban Population
(medium variant)

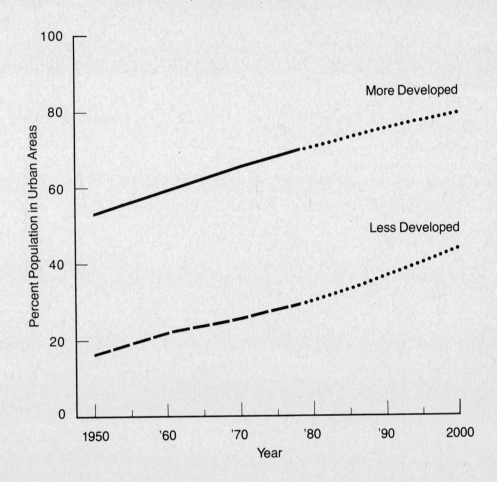

The projected trends spanning a century and a half in northern and southern groups of land masses reveal striking differences between the two in terms of population size. The northern and southern regions are grouped as follows:

Northern	Southern
North America	Latin America
Europe	Africa
U.S.S.R.	South Asia
East Asia	Oceania

In 1925, the northern group had a population of more than 1 billion and the southern group less than 1 billion. Their population growth curves crossed in the early 1970s, and the divergence is expected to continue even beyond the year 2075, when it is projected that there will be approximately 3 billion people in the northern group and 9 billion in the southern. These long-range estimates will, of course, be revised as present trends change.

It can be seen that both curves assume a sigmoid shape. According to this rather general estimate, the region of inflection in the northern group is in the 1970s, while inflection in the southern group will likely occur somewhat later, during the next 35 years, or after the turn of the century.

FIGURE 26

Population of the Northern and Southern Groups, 1925–2075

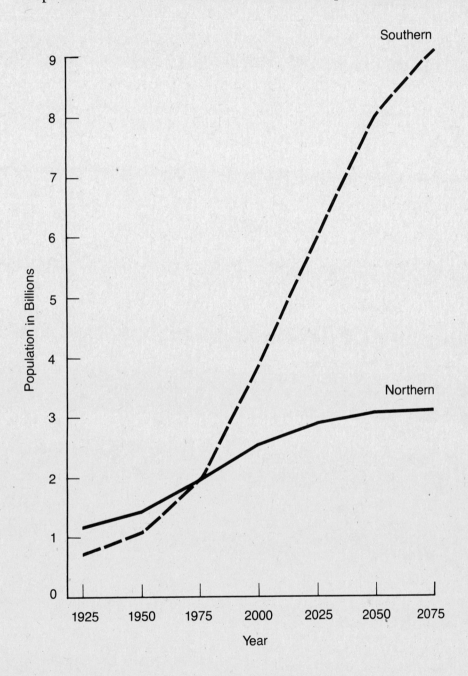

61

This figure describes population growth in the presently more and less developed regions over the period 1750 to 2200.° (It is to be noted that the grouping of populations on this page is not identical with those on the preceding page.) In 1880, the population of the "more developed" regions is estimated to have been approximately 250 million, while that of the "less developed" was over 700 million. By 1900, these numbers had changed to about 550 million and 1 billion, respectively. However, after the explosive growth of the present century, the expected plateau of population size (about 2100) will be approximately 1.4 billion in the more developed and over 9.1 billion in the less developed regions. If projections are correct, over 85 percent of world population will be in the presently less developed world.

In this figure, we again see the sigmoid shape of the curves and see that the region of inflection—of change from accelerating to decelerating growth—is occurring earlier in the more developed regions than in the developing regions.

°Distinction between "less" and "more" developed regions is not generally made for the period prior to the twentieth century. It is done here for illustrative purposes and for comparison with the other figures. For the period prior to 1950, data from North America, Europe, the U.S.S.R., Japan, and Oceania have been grouped under the designation "more developed," and the data from all remaining regions under "less developed." From 1950 on, the divisions made are the same as those in Figure 13.

FIGURE 27

Population of the More and Less Developed Regions, 1750–2200
(medium variant)

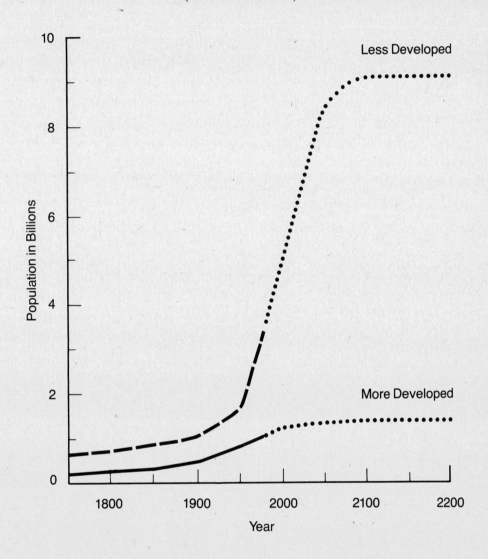

The accompanying figure shows the estimated increase in world population size in the period 1750 to 1975, with medium projections to the year 2200. This figure again illustrates the sigmoid pattern of human population growth and the estimated plateau at approximately 10.5 billion people. The high and low variants for the year 2125 are 14.2 and 8.0 billion respectively. The inflection of worldwide growth will become evident at about the turn of the century.

FIGURE 28

World Population Size, 1750–2200
(medium variant)

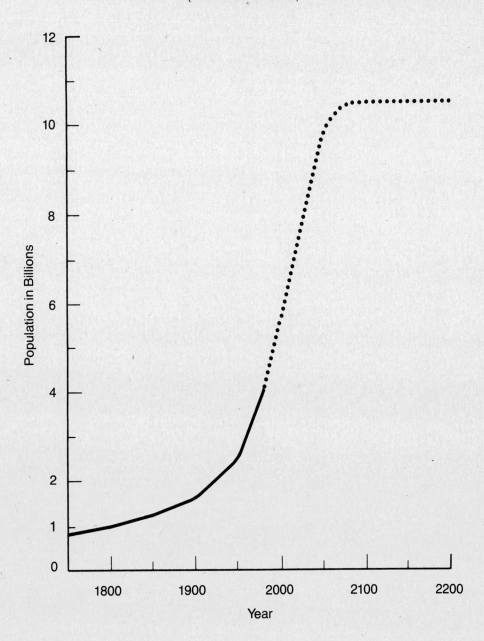

This final figure schematically describes the course of human population growth and population growth rates over a period extending from 8,000 years in the past to 8,000 years in the future. The curve indicates a plateau of world population at approximately 11 billion by the end of the twenty-first century and assumes that this level will remain stable or slowly decline.

If these estimates and assumptions are valid, we can see that the present extended period of rapid population growth is unique when seen from a long-range perspective; it has never occurred before and is unlikely to occur again.

FIGURE 29

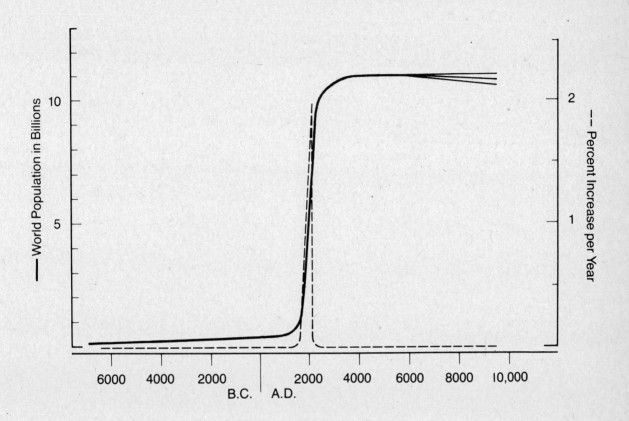

SUMMARY

In this section, we have seen many aspects of the course of population growth—population size, growth rates, birth and death rates, life expectancy, age distribution, male-female ratios, and other factors—all of which reveal sharp differences between the more and less developed regions. The projections presented here suggest, as inferred in Part I, that the human population growth curve will follow a sigmoid pattern. We are presently, in the last part of the twentieth century, entering the region of inflection of that curve.

Although we have turned a corner and the *rate* of world population growth is presently decreasing, world population *size* is still rapidly increasing and will continue to do so for many decades to come. The further slowing of growth will require expansion of family planning programs and a general increase in availability of social, health, and educational services. Even if such efforts are as successful as we hope, we will still face, in the coming decades, the enormous challenge, first, of providing for more people (and more people of advanced age) than have ever before been alive and, second, of adapting to conditions different from any we have faced.

The conditions of the future will be different from those of the recent past. The change from acceleration of growth to deceleration represents an epochal change in worldwide population trends. As this occurs, attitudes, values, and behavior may also shift.

This qualitative change will be the subject of Part III.

PART III

A New Epoch

The long-range course of human population growth can be divided schematically into three periods: first, very gradual increase in population size coinciding with pre- and early agricultural history; second, the present era, in which population is increasing rapidly and appears to be following a sigmoid trajectory; and third, the future, when it is projected that population size will remain relatively stable but at a much higher level.

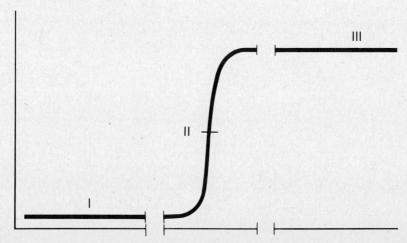

The second period has the characteristics of the sigmoid growth curves referred to earlier, and it can be seen to consist of two distinct portions: progressive acceleration and progressive deceleration in growth rate. We use the sigmoid curve not only to represent numbers of human beings but also to provide a frame of reference for discussing the nature of human values, attitudes, and behavior before and after the point of inflection.°

° We are using the sigmoid curve as an image of qualitative as well as of quantitative change over time but we have not labeled the axes. When the curves are used to reflect quantity, the horizontal axis indicates time and the vertical axis number. When the curves reflect qualitative differences, the horizontal axis reflects time and the vertical axis indicates changes in relative emphasis.

The sigmoid growth curve consists of two sections of different shape: the upturned portion describes a phase of progressive acceleration of growth; the second is downturned and describes a phase of progressive deceleration. The difference in shape between the two portions of the curve suggests both quantitative and qualitative differences in human life between the two periods of time. It not only indicates differences in population growth patterns but also suggests differences in the characteristics of prevailing conditions and in the quality of human life in the two periods.

FIGURE 30

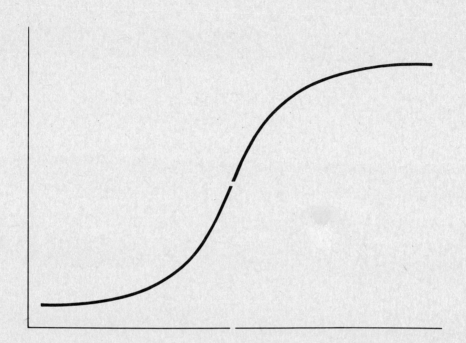

In this figure, the two parts of the curve before and after the point of inflection have been separated for emphasis. One is designated as A and the other as B. The periods of time prior to and following the point of inflection are referred to as Epoch A and Epoch B, respectively.

From the shape of the A curve, we might infer that, to someone born in Epoch A, the future would appear to be unlimited in terms of growth and expansion of, for example, population, resources, and availability of energy. To someone born in Epoch B, however, the future would seem to be a time of multiple limitations with a ceiling on growth and expansion. The difference in shape between the two curves thus implies that there will be a fundamental, qualitative difference in circumstances between the two periods of time.

FIGURE 31

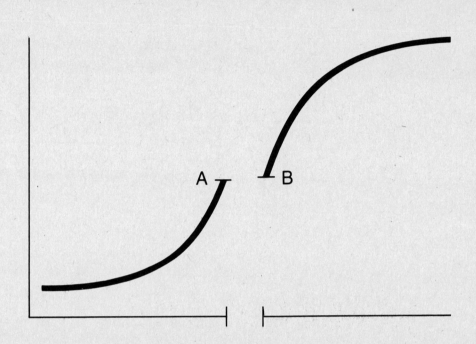

The difference in the circumstances between the two periods, implied by the shapes of the curves, also implies that the prevalent attitudes and value systems of the two epochs will be quite different.

This is suggested by the arrows indicating that what is of positive value in Epoch A could be expected to be of negative value in Epoch B.

In Epoch A, progressive increase in population size was seen to be of positive value, whereas, as we enter Epoch B, progressive increase is now of negative value. Specifically, many nations that previously tolerated or openly encouraged rapid population growth are now taking steps to check this growth. On the individual level, in many societies it was previously economically desirable to have large families; now, it is more desirable to limit family size.

FIGURE 32

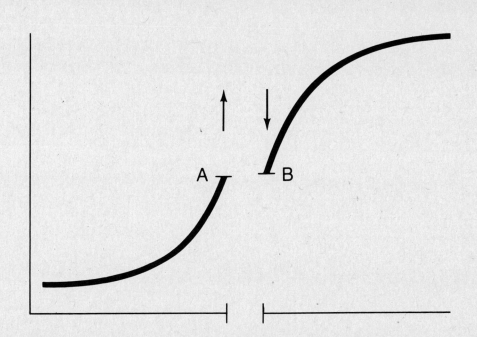

In this figure, other differences in values and atittudes can be seen.

During Epoch A, because mortality rates were high at all age levels, the control of disease and of premature death were of primary concern. Success in this regard has contributed to the recent sharp increase in population size. As a result of this, the concern in Epoch B can be expected to shift to the control of fertility and to a preoccupation with the enhancement of health.

FIGURE 33

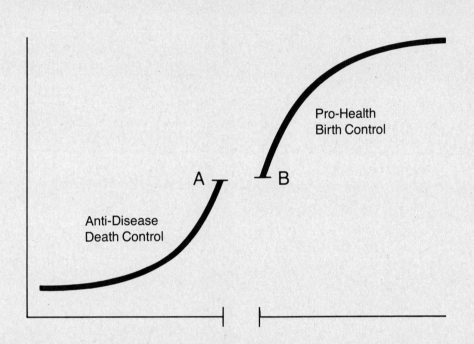

In Epoch A, there was an appropriate emphasis on quantity of children. In the changed conditions of Epoch B, in which fewer children will be born to each family, the emphasis can be expected to shift to the quality of care of children (see notes), the quality of each child's experience, and even to the overall quality of human life.

The decrease in growth of population may, in the long term, also result in an increase in concern with quality in such areas as education, food production, material production, and health care.

FIGURE 34

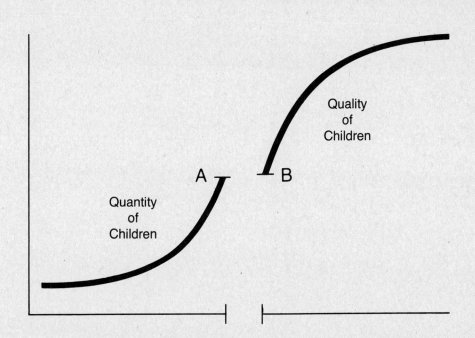

Quantity
of
Children

Quality
of
Children

A

B

The curves imply other differences in human life between the two epochs.

In Epoch A, growth was not constrained and those societies and industries that grew most rapidly tended to dominate. This was clearly evidenced in the period of exploration and colonization in the seventeenth, eighteenth, and nineteenth centuries and in the development of modern industrial nations. As a result, persistent growth and expansion have continued to be the dominant influence in modern social and economic life.

The shape of the second part of the curve suggests that in the different reality of Epoch B, an orientation toward dynamic equilibrium will be more appropriate than one toward persistent expansion. Population, material production, and consumption are expected to reach a plateau. This plateau, however, will not necessarily be a period of stagnation. It may well be a period of continuing change, development, and evolution in the human realm and of dynamic equilibrium in the material realm.

We are seeing the seeds of this shift today as individuals and groups throughout the world react to the growing awareness of limitation of available resources.

FIGURE 35

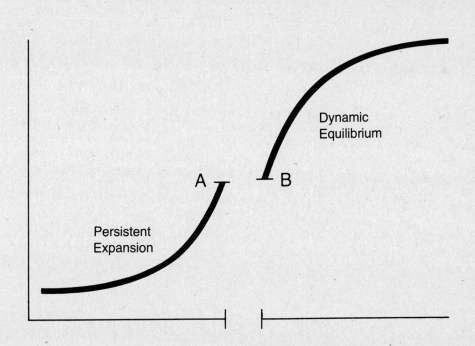

In Epoch A, a tendency toward extremes is inherent in the process of accelerating growth and change. Thus, excesses in growth and development and in the use of natural resources often occurred. In Epoch B, however, a tendency toward balance can be expected as an inherent part of the process of slowing growth, and balance will become evident both in relationships among human beings and in the relationship between human beings and nature.

For example, in the conditions of Epoch A, unrestricted use of natural resources was practiced. However, as conditions change, the excessive use of resources is unwise.

In the human realm, in periods of rapid growth, there is a tendency toward both excess and imbalance in distribution of wealth and resources. As the rate of growth diminishes, reduction of extremes and increase in balance will advantageously affect the presently rich as well as the presently poor, but in different ways.

FIGURE 36

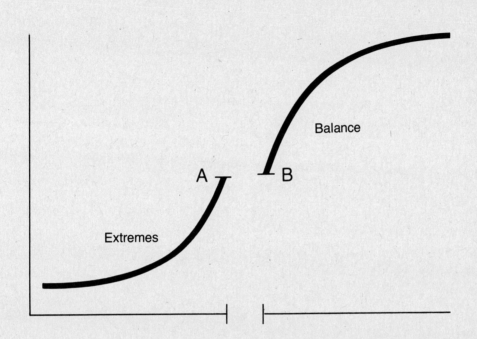

In a similar fashion, we can expect a shift in other orientations or attitudes. As indicated in the diagram, competition, independence, and power tended to dominate in Epoch A. In the conditions of Epoch B, however, collaboration, interdependence, and consensus may prove to be of higher value in providing for basic human needs.

Several instances of the beginning of this shift can be seen. For example, nations around the Mediterranean, understanding their mutual interest in environmental quality, have, in recent years, found it important to collaborate in their efforts to check pollution and to preserve the quality of those waters. Through negotiation and consensus, they have reached a mutual agreement on strategies and guidelines for control.

At a more local level, increase in the participation of workers in management decisions, most notably in Japan and in some U.S. factories, also suggests a trend toward collaboration, interdependence, and reliance on consensus in industrial organization.

FIGURE 37

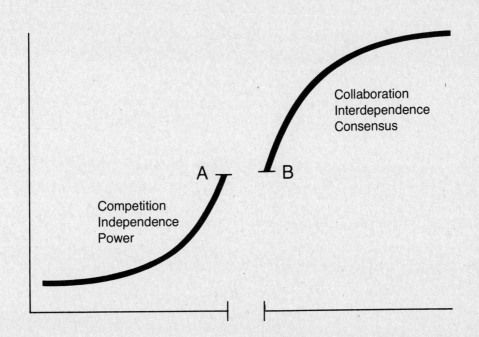

Competition
Independence
Power

Collaboration
Interdependence
Consensus

In Epoch A, competition and the demands of persistent, accelerating growth were inherently associated with either/or attitudes and philosophies and the prevalence of win-lose strategies in human relationships. However, the tendency toward balance, collaboration, and interdependence in Epoch B may be based upon and evoke a philosophy of both/and and the development of win-win strategies.

In the latter set of orientations, both sides gain something and both sides relinquish something. Neither one loses all or wins all. This is in contrast to the prevalent attitudes of Epoch A in which conflicts often ended with one side winning and the other side losing.

An example of a both/and attitude may be seen in international relationships among countries that are interdependent in the production of food and use of natural resources. In such a situation, increased productivity of one nation is, in reality, of benefit to both. With an either/or attitude, one would regard a gain to the other as a loss to itself.

Other examples of both/and thinking are illustrated in the following sections.

FIGURE 38

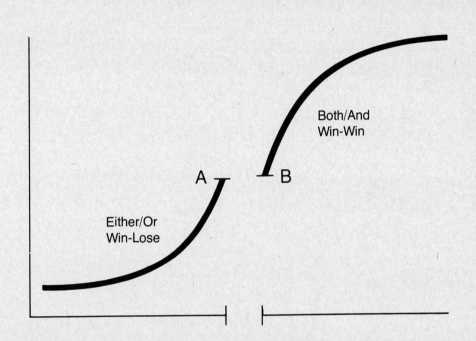

In Epoch A, the short-range costs or benefits of actions were of greater concern than the long-range. Orientation was to the present, and situations, actions, or effects of actions were usually seen in isolation, as parts unrelated to other human groups or ecological systems. In Epoch B, higher population density and greater demands on the physical environment will necessitate taking broader, more long-range effects into account.

One example of this is seen in the effects of disposal of wastes. In the early phases of industrial development, the adverse effects of waste either were not perceived or could safely be ignored. In Epoch B, however, in part because of increased density of population and increased production of waste, the consideration of such adverse effects will be essential. Avoidance or amelioration of pollution will be in the interests both of neighboring populations (either human or other species) and of those who may be producing the waste.

This shift in attitudes is reflected in the increased concern with pollution in both developed and developing nations.

FIGURE 39

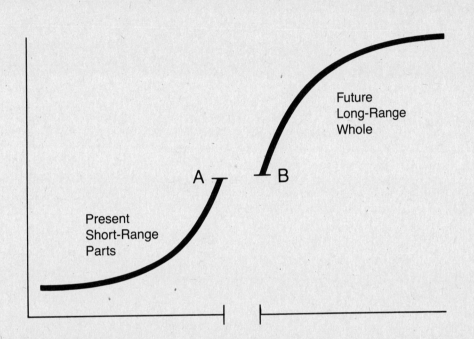

Present
Short-Range
Parts

Future
Long-Range
Whole

The final figure in Part III is intended to underscore the nature and significance of the change that is occurring in our time and to justify the view of the emergence of a new reality in the history of humankind.

A major shift in our perception of reality occurred in the past when a prior belief that the earth was flat was altered by evidence that the earth was round. Another similar shift occurred when the belief that the sun revolved around the earth was changed by the discovery that the earth revolves around the sun. These changes in our relationship to earth and to sun were changes in perception and not changes in reality; the realities were not altered, only our perception of them.

Now, however, another major change is in the making. This is a change from seeing the world as limitless in terms of growth to seeing it as limited. It is also a change from seeing ourselves in opposition to each other to seeing ourselves in collaboration with one another. It is due not only to a change in perception but to a necessary change in human attitudes and spirit that comes in response to a change in reality, as expressed by the shapes of the curves. The change from A to B can be seen in our relationships to nature, our relationships to each other, and in our relationships to ourselves.

FIGURE 40

Relationship of

Man to Earth

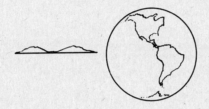

Man to Sun

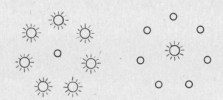

Man to Man

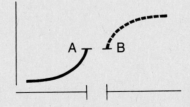

Summary

The figures in this section have suggested that a major shift is occurring in the quality of human values, attitudes, behavior, and relationships.

This brings us to the realization that individually and collectively we share the responsibility for the future course of events on the planet, whether it be positive or negative. This outcome depends upon the way in which we respond to the new reality of population growth and of available resources. The images presented here suggest the possibility, as well as the necessity, of responding to these changes in a positive and humane way.

Just as shifts in population growth patterns occur over time, qualitative shifts in attitudes, values, and behavior, like those suggested in Part III, will take place over a long period of time—at least several human generations. We are only now entering this crucial period of change, and much of the transition lies ahead. Some of the many paradoxes and conflicts in this difficult period will be presented in Part IV.

PART IV

Paradox and Conflict

Human beings possess the capacity for a wide range of attitudes and behavior. The idea underlying the preceding discussion is that those attitudes and behavior that are advantageous and therefore appropriate under one set of circumstances (the reality of Epoch A) may be disadvantageous and inappropriate under another (the reality of Epoch B).

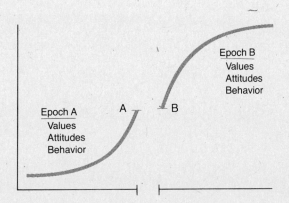

The context or circumstances that prevail determine which attitudes and behavior are appropriate at different times. Thus the emergence of Epoch B values outlined in Part III is seen as a necessary response to the different reality of that era.

In the region of inflection growth rates are highest, acceleration is changing to deceleration, and values are shifting most rapidly. This period can be expected to be a time of increased conflict. In the following section, we will look more closely at the paradoxes and conflicts associated with this period.

101

As we have seen, attitudes, values, strategies, and behavior that are appropriate under the circumstances of Epoch A are likely to be inappropriate in Epoch B and vice versa. This figure compares the relative advantage or relative value, in Epochs A and B, of Epoch A-type with Epoch B-type qualities. The diagram suggests that, in the period associated with the first part of the curve, Epoch A-type responses are more advantageous to people and to society while Epoch B-type responses are more advantageous in the second. The converse is also true.

The change in values outlined in Part III can therefore be seen as the result of learning and adaptation in response to this change.

FIGURE 41

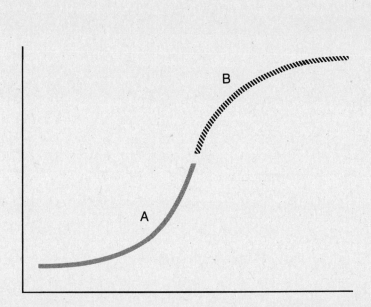

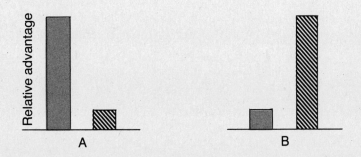

Relative advantage of A-type attitudes and behavior

Relative advantage of B-type attitudes and behavior

As seen below, the attitudes, values, and behavior that serve self-interest in Epoch A are very different from those that do so in Epoch B.

Epoch A	Epoch B
Individual	Individual and Group
Power	Consensus
Competition	Collaboration
Independence	Interdependence
Extremes	Balance
Part	Whole
Either/Or	Both/And

Paradoxically, this means that in the reality of Epoch B, behaving in a more generous, community-oriented manner will better serve the self-interest of both individuals and groups than behaving in an exclusively self-oriented, competitive way. Therefore, collaboration, awareness of others, and balance will not be regarded as personal sacrifice; instead, they will be personally and collectively beneficial.

FIGURE 42

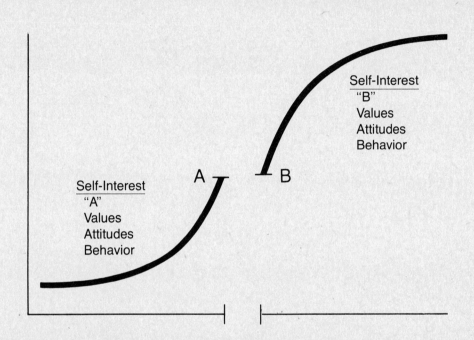

In the context of Epoch A, the generous or humane attitudes appropriate to Epoch B are qualities not often perceived as pragmatic. However, in the different reality of Epoch B, such strategies will be *both* pragmatic *and* humane.

For example, improvement in the quality of life in the developing regions and the self-sufficiency of those nations will benefit both the people in these areas and those in the more developed world. As mentioned in Part II, improvements in health care, education, and economic viability in the less developed areas will help in ameliorating population pressures, which would benefit the world as a whole. In addition, a balanced relationship of wealth and exchange would lead to more economic and political stability in all regions. In Epoch A, such changes might not have been perceived as beneficial to the more developed areas; they are now being seen as advantageous to all regions.

FIGURE 43

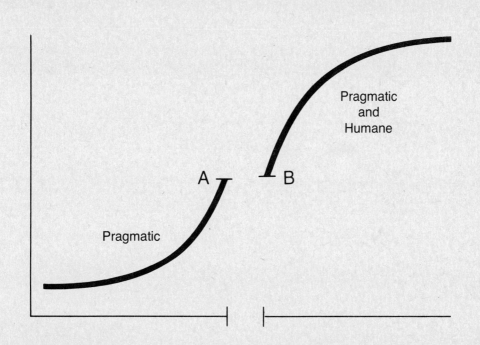

In the region of inflection, the relative advantages of Epoch A- and Epoch B-type responses are rapidly changing, and they tend to be more balanced than at other points on the curve. When this is true, there will be conflict between those who hold to Epoch A–related values, such as continued expansion, competition, and a view of parts, and those who hold to Epoch B–related values, such as balance, collaboration, and a view of whole systems.

An example of this can be seen in the use of resources and the related problem of disposal of wastes.

At the inflection point, one would expect confrontations between those who emphasize the benefits of unconstrained use of resources and production of waste, a view that was previously appropriate, and those who emphasize the benefits of moderation in consumption and the amelioration of pollution, a view that will be appropriate in the future. This conflict will be apparent both between groups holding different positions and within those that make decisions regarding planning and development.

Similar examples of areas of probable conflict are family size, industrial expansion, and the benefits of formation of collaborative relationships.

FIGURE 44

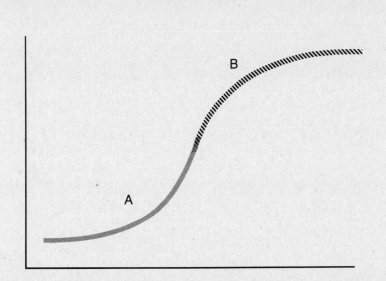

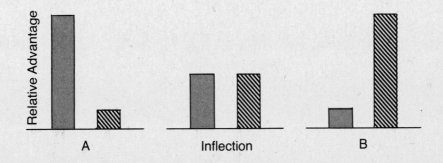

Relative advantage of persistent development without amelioration of pollution.

Relative advantage of slow development with amelioration of pollution.

109

The region of inflection is seen as the time of transition from the predominance of A values to that of B values. In this figure, the relative position of the two lines° indicates that Epoch B values exist even in the period before inflection, but are less dominant than Epoch A values. In Epoch B, the relative dominance is reversed. As indicated, the tendency of one set of values to persist as the other begins to emerge will give rise to tension, conflict, and uncertainty.

The image on the opposite page offers an explanation for the tension we feel at this time. It suggests that the conflicts are an inherent part of this developmental and evolutionary process. They are not necessarily a signal of an impending end of the human species but reflect the process of inversion that is now occurring.

° In this and the following figure, the vertical axis indicates relative emphasis and the interrelationship of sets of attitudes, values, and behavior. The horizontal axis still refers to time.

FIGURE 45

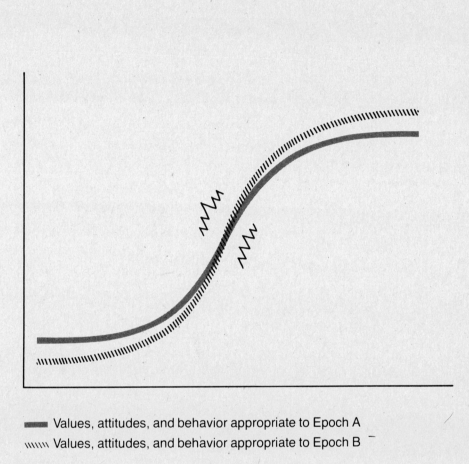

▬▬ Values, attitudes, and behavior appropriate to Epoch A

\\\\\ Values, attitudes, and behavior appropriate to Epoch B

In the process of adapting to changing conditions, conflict may be most effectively resolved, as symbolized here, with a both/and approach. For example, completely discarding the technological and social developments of Epoch A in an effort to immediately halt growth would be inappropriate and unrealizable. On the other hand, attempting to resolve tensions by completely suppressing the tendencies of Epoch B would be equally disadvantageous. With a both/and approach, the developments that have been part of Epoch A can be combined with Epoch B values in order to develop solutions that are appropriate to changing conditions.

A specific example of this might be the simultaneous short-term reliance on nonrenewable resources of energy with the long-term goal of reducing consumption and of developing efficient means for using renewable resources.

FIGURE 46

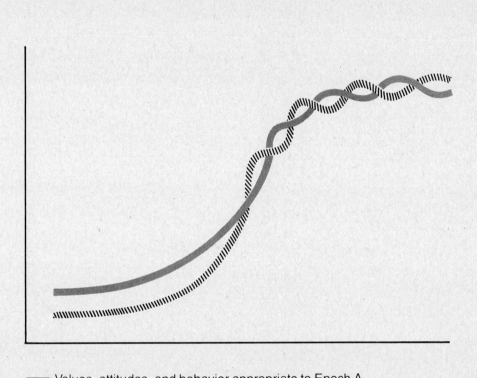

━━━ Values, attitudes, and behavior appropriate to Epoch A

ᴧᴧᴧᴧᴧ Values, attitudes, and behavior appropriate to Epoch B

Over an extended period of time, with the dominance of both/and attitudes, the Epoch A to Epoch B transformation can be seen as a series of reconciliations of opposing tendencies in a continuing process, as suggested in the
upper figure. Conflicting tendencies are apparent but their synthesis is facilitat-
ed by both/and strategies. Bringing about this kind of resolution is one of the
great challenges of the present era. Successes in this respect will result in the
evolution of new ways of life that will be beneficial to both individuals and
groups and to the furthering of human evolution.

On the other hand, the continued dominance of either/or attitudes would
lead, over a period of time, to an escalation rather than a reduction of conflicts.
In time, this would lead to widespread conflict, famine, war, and, possibly, to a
total collapse of the human population.

FIGURE 47

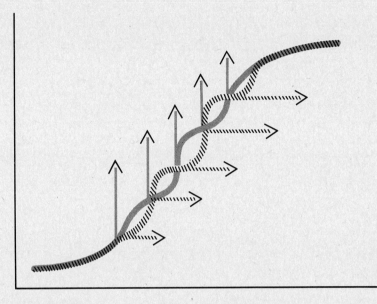

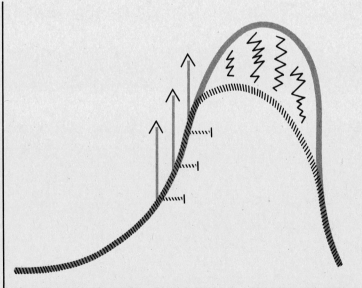

Epoch A trends

Epoch B trends

When viewed from a short-term perspective, as represented in the upper figure, the tension and conflict inherent in this transition may seem chaotic and symptomatic of a disintegrating, collapsing world. However, when viewed from a longer-range perspective, as provided by the sigmoid curve in the lower figure, these conflicts and uncertainties can be seen as part of an orderly if somewhat difficult process of nature. Looked at in this way, the disturbances of the present time may be seen not as a symptom of a disease that must be treated or eradicated but as a result of the obsolesence of formerly successful patterns of life and the uncertain beginnings of new patterns appropriate to the emerging conditions.

FIGURE 48

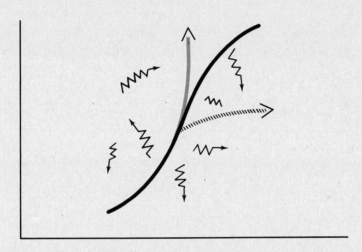

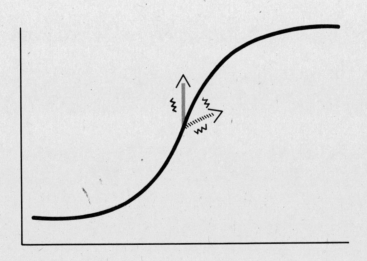

▬▬ Epoch A trends

\\\\\ Epoch B trends

Summary

In this section, we have suggested that Epoch B values, attitudes, and behavior are beginning to emerge not only because they are humane, but because they are advantageous to the individual and to society. During this transition, it can be expected that conflict, at all levels of human life, will increase. In the long term, such conflicts will be most effectively and constructively resolved with both/and rather than either/or strategies.

The present period is especially sensitive. In resisting change, we may hold to values that are obsolete and exceed the tolerance of nature to endure what has lost its usefulness. Resisting change may ameliorate some problems in the short term, but will not provide the basic change in values needed in this epochal transition. Strategies that resist change also greatly increase the risk of disaster through famine or nuclear war.

Though the present period of crisis confronts us with the danger of self-extinction, it also presents us with an opportunity for development that could aid long-term survival of the human species and enchance the quality of individual life. If this does occur, it will be through the creativity, initiative, and shared responsibility of individuals throughout the world and through the successful reconciliation of conflicting tendencies.

PART V

Reconciliation

Though the emphasis in the discussion up to this point has been on values, attitudes, and behavior of individuals and of large groups such as nations or groups of nations, it is understood that these are influenced by social institutions, political organization, and economic relationships. Therefore, change in all realms will occur with the emergence of new values. In accord with this, a view of human biological and social existence is emerging, one in which the biological nature of human beings, individual and sociocultural values, and institutional structure are not considered in isolation from one another but as interrelated parts of a whole.

In the process of the evolution of attitudes and of social forms appropriate to the new epoch, presently conflicting and divergent aspects of life will converge and be reconciled. In this concluding section, we will return to a long-range view of human population growth, give some illustrations of divergence, convergence, and reconciliation, and, finally, present an integrated view of the complexity of human phenomena.

The figure at the right depicts human population growth from 8000 B.C. to the present. It can readily be seen that the greater part of human history has been in conditions of relatively slow population increase—increase far less rapid than we have experienced in the last several hundred years.

FIGURE 49

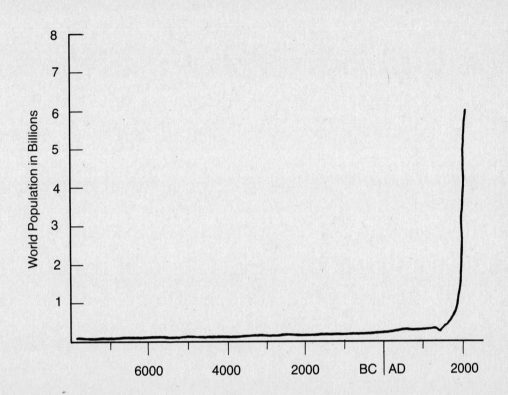

This figure is an extension of the previous one, showing human population size over a period extending 8,000 years into the past and an equal period into the future.* From this perspective, we see that the present period of rapid change is unique with respect to the long-term future as well as to the remote past.

* The graph of the future shown here assumes a stabilization of population growth within the next 100 years, with approximate equilibrium or slow decline over an indeterminant period. Long-term projections of population growth are unreliable at best, and the path pictured here may be considerably different from what will emerge. Nevertheless, the image presented here does provide a context for viewing the present era.

FIGURE 50

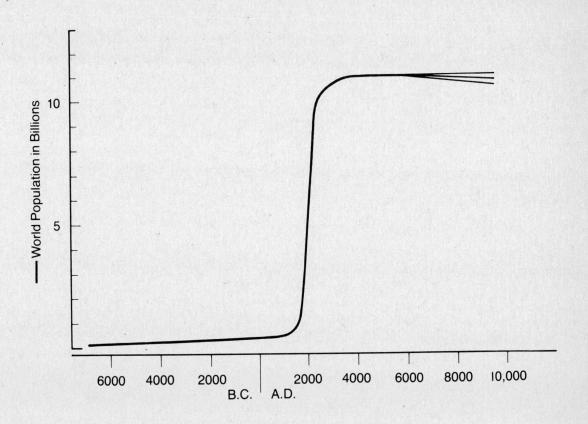

The uniqueness of our present period is further emphasized by this long-term view of population growth rates, which reveals a startingly sharp peak in the present era.

FIGURE 51

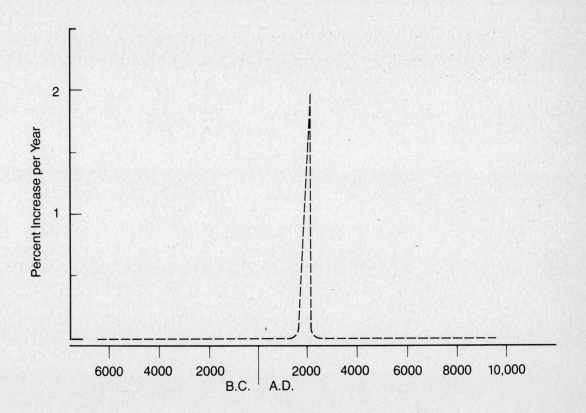

This figure, which combines the previous two, completes the image of the present era when seen in the long-range context of population growth.

The human species is experiencing far more rapid and sustained change in terms of population growth and sociocultural development than has occurred before or is likely to occur in the future.

Intuitively, we sense from this image that, from a psychological and social standpoint, human beings may be better adapted to conditions associated with less rapid change (like those that existed in the more distant past and that are anticipated in the coming centuries) than they are to those that we presently experience.

FIGURE 52

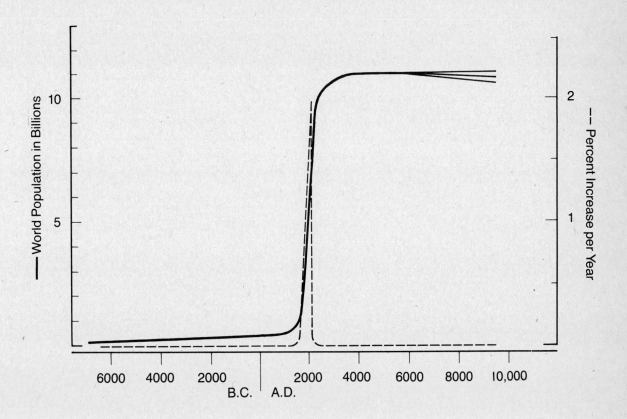

As mentioned earlier, the population curve may be viewed as consisting, schematically, of three sections: one, a period of very slow growth; two, the present period of rapid change; and three, a future period of relatively slow change but with a much larger world population.

Some of the characteristics of the three periods are listed in the table below the figure. It is interesting to note that, because of the large population size and the development of technology, life in Period III may be similar, in ways, to present experience. However, in other ways, such as low growth rates, awareness of environmental limits, and tendency toward equilibrium, some of the qualities of life in the far future will resemble those that existed in Period I of the curve more than those of Period II.

This figure gives rise to the idea that our adaptations to the future may be the result of the reemergence of qualities of life that predominated in the distant past and their integration with those that have recently prevailed.

FIGURE 53

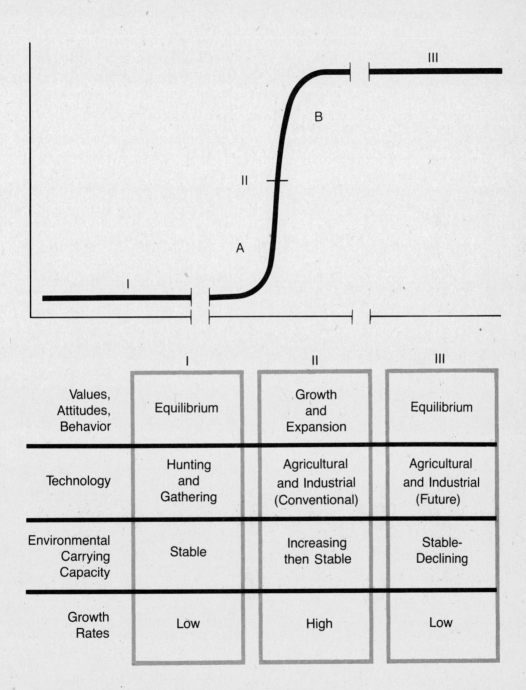

	I	II	III
Values, Attitudes, Behavior	Equilibrium	Growth and Expansion	Equilibrium
Technology	Hunting and Gathering	Agricultural and Industrial (Conventional)	Agricultural and Industrial (Future)
Environmental Carrying Capacity	Stable	Increasing then Stable	Stable-Declining
Growth Rates	Low	High	Low

The patterns revealed in the preceding figures suggest that differing tendencies that have always been present in human beings have diverged in the course of the rapid changes of more recent history. The image on the opposite page° suggests that, coinciding with the epochal changes occurring at the present time, this pattern of divergence is shifting to one of convergence and of integration.

In the following figures, examples of this phenomenon will be presented.

° As in Figures 45 and 46, the vertical axis represents the relative emphasis, or dominance of, and the interrelationship between the states, characteristics, disciplines, or ways of thinking indicated on the diagrams. The horizontal axis refers to time.

FIGURE 54

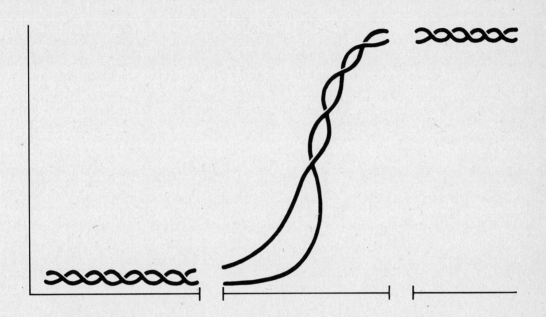

In the period to come, an increase in the cultural and economic influence of the developing areas and a relative decrease in the dominance of the developed nations can be expected. This is indicated both by the disproportionate increase in population in the developing regions and by the progressive tendency toward worldwide interdependence in the period to come.

In the developing regions, the interaction of technology and economics of the developed regions with social and cultural patterns of preindustrial societies offers the prospect for the emergence of new types of social organization that would incorporate the most appropriate aspects of life in both worlds. Such developments would be of value to people in all regions.

FIGURE 55

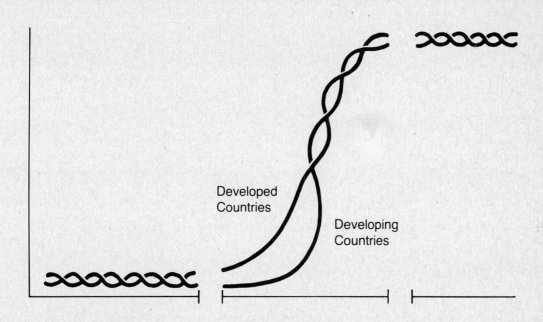

Developed
Countries

Developing
Countries

A similar phenomenon can be expected to occur in the economic realm. At present, the tendency to make decisions based purely on material costs and benefits are in conflict with the tendency to base decisions on human considerations, such as quality of individual health or the quality of the physical environment. In contrast, economic decisions in the future will increasingly take into account both human and material value. This change will affect the nature of economic relationships and organization in the years ahead.

FIGURE 56

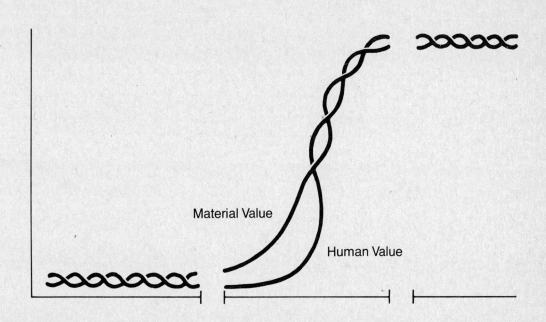

Material Value

Human Value

In the future, with both a high population density and increased emphasis on the quality of individual life, forms of political organization may emerge that are responsive to the needs both of individuals and large groups. Thus, a need is now emerging for integrating local, small-scale organizations, which provide for the political, cultural, and material needs of the individual, with large-scale, centralized organizations concerned with communication among groups and with coordination of efforts to meet human needs.

FIGURE 57

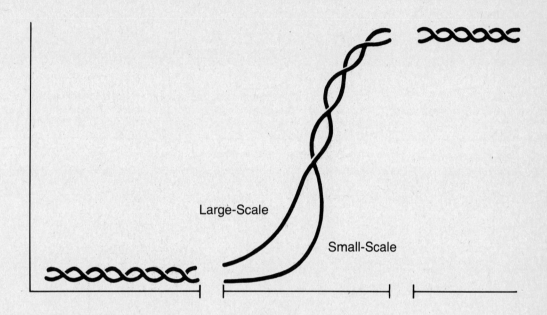

In recent times, especially deep conflicts have arisen between what is called the modern way of life and the traditional. As is pictured here, a resolution of this conflict will be necessary.

In time to come, we are likely to experience a reconciliation of old and new in the creation of traditions appropriate to the emerging reality. While traditions that were appropriate to former times have been rejected in the course of modernization, many of the elements of these older cultures will be essential, in combination with those of the present, in the creation of altogether new traditions for the future.

FIGURE 58

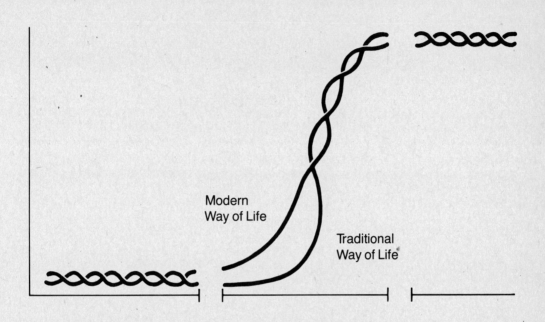

Modern
Way of Life

Traditional
Way of Life

In recent years there has been a rapprochement of the perspective and orientation of Western thought with that of the Eastern world. As pictured here, this coming together can be anticipated to continue.

FIGURE 59

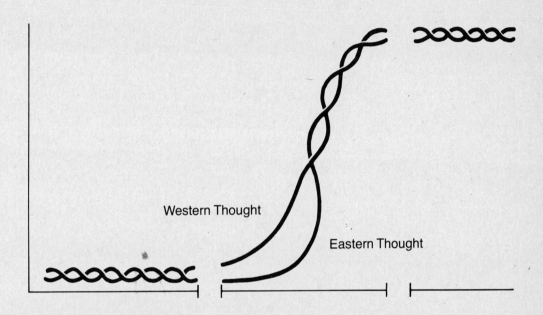

Western Thought

Eastern Thought

There has also been a long-standing distinction and, sometimes, antagonism between the realms of science and art. In the coming years, we may see a gradual convergence of the experience, as well as the knowledge and insight, generated in these two essential human endeavors.

FIGURE 60

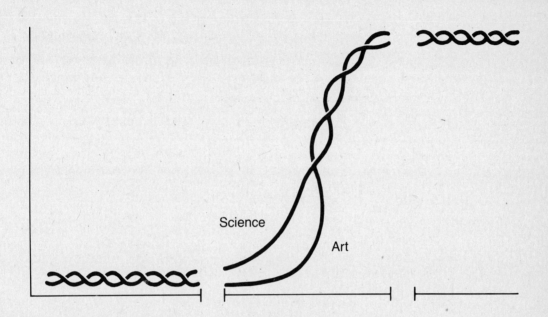

The process of convergence will also bring about reconciliation among the major intellectual disciplines: the humanities and the natural and social sciences. In the process, an evolutionary view that incorporates the ecological, biological, social, mental, and creative aspects of human existence will gradually emerge.

FIGURE 61

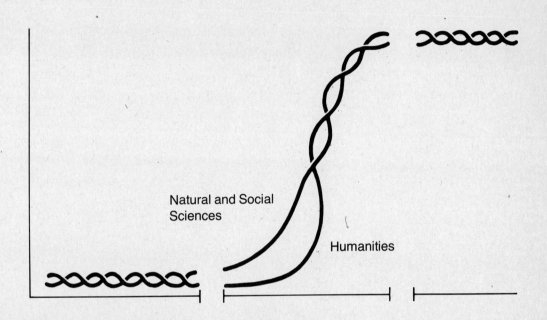

Natural and Social
Sciences

Humanities

The changes in human values and in human life outlined here will be associated with *both* individual *and* institutional change. Change in both will occur, for change in either will necessarily alter the other in the process of the fundamental change through which humankind is now passing.

This kind of broad and basic change will therefore permeate every facet of human existence. It will affect work and community relationships as well as political, social, and economic organizations. It will also involve family relationships, cultural patterns, and the mental and physical state of individual human beings.

FIGURE 62

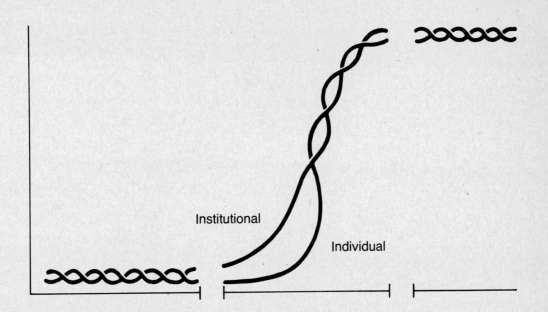

A comprehensive view, as seen in this and the subsequent figures, will be needed in the coming years. This diagram schematically indicates that there is a need for consideration of details in the continuum from the molecular level to the ecological. An approach to human problems now requires attention and understanding of not just one, but all levels, and solutions will require knowledge in all realms.

FIGURE 63

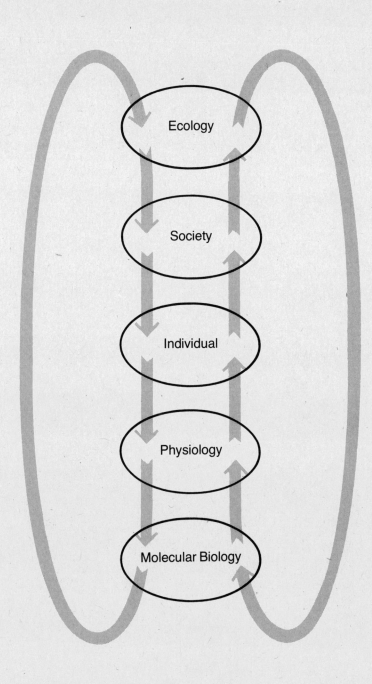

A diagram of a comprehensive view of the complex factors involved in human life is presented in this and the following figures.

At the center, we have placed "bioevolution" in order to emphasize that the nature of the individual and of society is determined, in part, by biological and evolutionary forces. The individual enters the social process not as a *tabula rasa*, but as a member of the human species, carrying propensities and predispositions shaped by a long and continuing evolutionary process. This is not intended to suggest that all of human behavior is fixed at conception by genetic factors; as we shall see in the following figures, the individual does not exist in isolation, but is influenced by a rich context of diverse social systems, beliefs, and individual human differences. This figure merely emphasizes that biology and evolution should be taken into consideration in understanding human beings and human society.

FIGURE 64

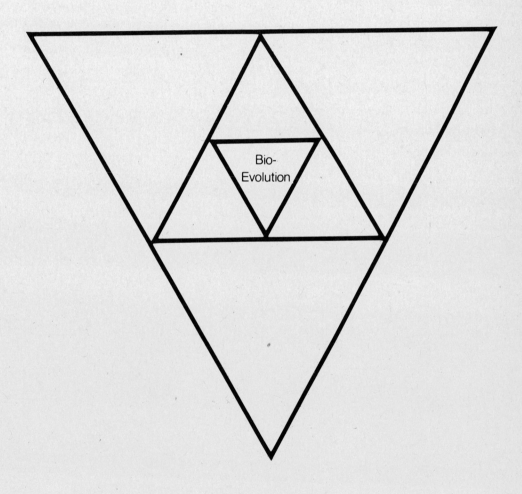

Attitudes, values, and behavior, which have been the focus of this essay, are created by the interaction of the individual with the wider sociocultural system that forms the emotional, intellectual, and material context in which the individual develops.

To represent this, we have added to the figure those societal factors that most directly interact with individuals: institutions, including the family, involved in education and socialization; those concerned with the formation of cultural and religious beliefs; and the occupational/socioeconomic context of each individual or family. These are all part of the social environment that is both shaped by and, in turn, shapes individuals.

FIGURE 65

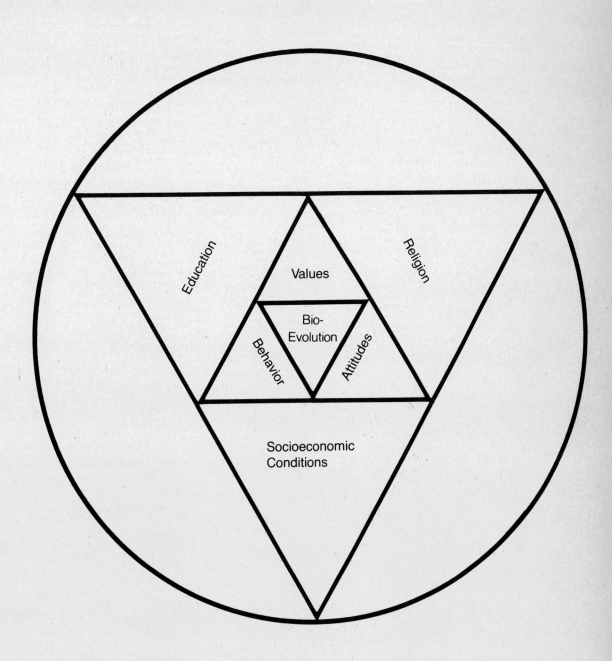

The elements referred to on the previous page exist within the context of the still larger social, political, and economic organization of society, as indicated on the outer part of the figure. The entire complex—biological, social, and institutional—can now be seen as an interrelated whole. However, this whole must be seen in the still larger context of the physical environment. Like all biological systems, human systems exist within the limitations and the opportunities inherent in the natural environment.

When human life is seen in this ecological context, the focus can return to the center of the diagram, and can now be shifted back and forth from the center to the periphery, revealing the interrelationship of all of the biological, social, institutional, and ecological factors that influence and are influenced by human life.

FIGURE 66

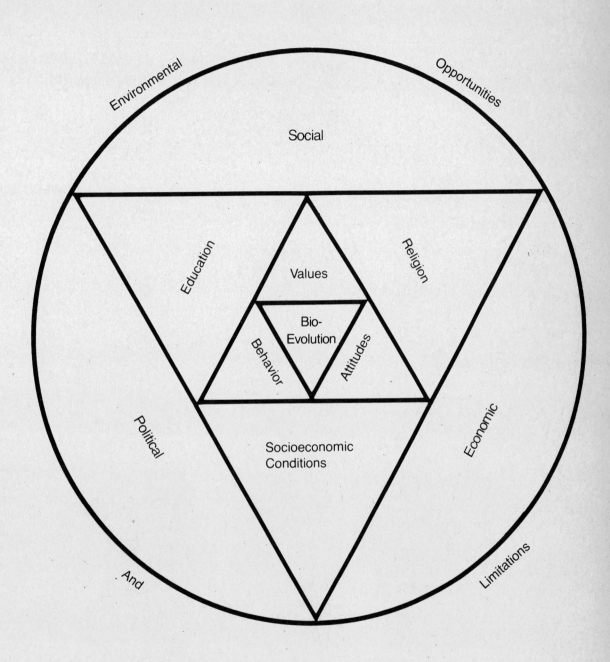

Summary

The epochal change now taking place affects every aspect of human life—individual and institutional, emotional and cognitive, personal and technological. It calls for the reconciliation of imbalances and conflicts that have arisen in the course of preceding decades and even centuries.

The reconciliations will occur in ways that will differ according to local history, culture, and ecological conditions. Through the human capacity for creativity, through variation among human beings and human societies, and through a process of evolution, the scientific and technological developments of recent centuries can be reconciled with values essential to human survival on the planet. Whether we will successfully make this transition remains to be seen, but the images presented here suggest our capacity to do so.

If we exercise that capability, we have the opportunity to prolong the survival and evolution of the human species (and of life on this planet) and, in the process, qualitively to improve the present level of human health, well-being, and satisfaction.

Epilogue

The epochal transformation described in these pages is occurring through a myriad of small changes at every level of human life. As conditions change, each generation is born into circumstances that are different from those experienced by the preceding one. Through different experiences, each develops different viewpoints and different values. Over a period of time, as values change, so will relationships and, with them, institutions. The challenge that we presently face in adapting to the future is to allow new values to emerge and to modify institutions appropriately.

Even though the charts and diagrams suggest that, in the long term, the course of the epochal change is predetermined, it is not. It is subject to our influence. Successful adaptations will require human effort, creativity, and innovation. As values change, all aspects of life from personal roles to the basic assumptions or structure of political and economic systems will be modified.

As population growth slows and as we approach a plateau in world population size, our greatest challenges lie in the human and social realm. Human and social challenges—improving quality of life, feeding billions of people, avoiding the disastrous depletion of resources, creating societies that meet the material and cultural needs of the individual—challenges that now seem insurmountable, may in time be no more insoluble than previously "impossible" challenges—development of heavier-than-air flight, modern agriculture, electronics, space travel.

Previously, necessity demanded the solution of technological problems. Now as we enter a new and different reality, the demand of necessity is for the solution of problems involving human values, attitudes, behavior, and social institutions.

At this point, innovation in the area of human development and social relationships is as important as the advent of agriculture 10,000 years ago, or the understanding of microbes and machines in the past century. Just as some of the brightest minds of recent years turned their attention to the advancement of science and technology and to the prevention and cure of disease, many of the brightest minds of coming generations will turn their attention to the phenomena of the human mind and the improvement of the quality of human life.

In a sense, we are on a frontier, but it is not territorial or technological; it is human and social. In this period of changing conditions and values, doubts arise as to our ability to cross this frontier and to meet the demands of the future. We will, in the process of responding to the forces and limits of nature, learn whether we have the capacity to meet this challenge. If we do, then we will emerge from the present period not merely as survivors, but as human beings in a new reality.

Notes

PART I

Figure 1. Adapted from John McHale, *The Future of the Future* (New York: Braziller, 1969), Fig. 1, p. 58. (By permission of the publisher, George Braziller, Inc.) Data point for 1980 from United Nations, *World Population Trends and Prospects by Country, 1950–2000: Summary Report of the 1978 Assessment*, ST/ESA/SER.R/ 33 (New York, 1979), Table 1, p. 4.

Figure 4. Raymond Pearl, *The Biology of Population Growth* (New York: Knopf, 1925). (Copyright 1925 by Alfred A. Knopf, Inc. and renewed 1953 by Maude de Witt Pearl. Reprinted by permission of Alfred A. Knopf, Inc.) Fig. 12, p. 35.

Figure 5. *Ibid.*, Fig. 4, p. 9.

Figure 6. Adapted from Oscar W. Richards, "Potentially Unlimited Multiplication of Yeast with Constant Environment and Limiting of Growth by Changing Environment," *Journal of General Physiology* 11 (1928): 525–538, Fig. 4, p. 534. (By permission.)

Figure 7. J. Davidson, "On the Growth of the Sheep Population in Tasmania," *Transactions of the Royal Society of South Australia* 62, no. 2 (December 23, 1938): 342–346, Fig. 1, p. 344. (By permission.)

Figure 8. Communications Research Machines, Inc., *Biology Today* (Del Mar, Calif.: CRM Books, 1972), Fig. 33.6, p. 661. (By permission of copyright holder, Random House, Inc.)

Figure 9. Schematic drawing adapted from Jean van der Tak, Carl Haub, and Elaine Murphy, "Our Population Predicament: A New Look," *Population Bulletin* 34, no. 5 (December 1979), Fig. 1, p. 2. Data for number of years for population to increase by 1 billion, *Ibid.*, Table 4, p. 4.

PART II

Figure 10. Van der Tak, Haub, and Murphy, "Our Population Predicament," *Population Bulletin* 34, no. 5 (December 1979), Fig. 1, p. 2. (By permission.)

Figure 11. Data for 1 A.D. and 1650 A.D. from midpoint of ranges given in United Nations, "The Determinants and Consequences of Population Trends: New Summary of Findings on Interaction of Demographic, Economic and Social Factors, Volume I," *Population Studies* no. 50 (1973), Table II.1, p. 10.

Data for 1750–1900 from John D. Durand, "The Modern Expansion of World Population," *Proceedings of the American Philosophical Society* 111, no. 3 (June 1967): 136–159, Table 1, p. 137.

Data for 1950–1980 from United Nations, *World Population Trends and Prospects by Country, 1950–2000,* Tables 1–A and 1–B.

Figure 12. Data from United Nations, *World Population Trends and Prospects by Country, 1950–2000,* Tables 1–A and 1–B.

Figure 13, Data from United Nations, *Selected Demographic Indicators by Country 1950–2000; Demographic Estimates and Projections as Assessed in 1978,* ST/ESA/SER.R/38 (New York, 1980), pp. 12–13.

Figure 14. *Ibid.*

Figure 15. Data from the 1981 World Population Data Sheet of the Population Reference Bureau, prepared by Carl Haub, Population Reference Bureau, Washington, D.C. (April 1981)

Figure 16 (text). There has been a notable drop in fertility in many developing nations in recent years. See Sir Maurice Kendall, "The World Fertility Survey: Current Status and Findings," *Population Reports,* Series M, no. 3 (Baltimore: Population Information Program, The Johns Hopkins University, July 1979).

One of the reasons for this decline appears to be that, as a society develops, children spend more time in school, contribute less to family work and income, and, therefore, become more of an economic burden to parents. See "Fertility Drop: Turning a Corner," *Science News* 113, no. 8 (February 25, 1978): 116–117.

Figure 16. Data from United Nations, *Selected Demographic Indicators by Country 1950–2000,* pp. 12–13.

Figure 17 (text). The suggestion that education, health services, and decline in infant mortality may be important in the reduction of fertility is summarized briefly by Rafael M. Salas in "The State of World Population, 1978" and "The State of World Population, 1980," introductions to the Annual Report on UNFPA Activities and Plans. For another example, see also T. N. Krishnan, "Socio-economic Policies: Some Case Histories, Part I: Kerala," in Dick MacDonald (ed.), *The Population Story; From Now to 2000* (London, Ontario: Western Journalism Library, 1979), Chap. 8.

Figure 17. All data except singulate mean age at marriage from T. N. Krishnan, "Socio-economic Factors Affecting Fertility Decline in Sri Lanka and Kerala," paper delivered at "Developments and Trends in World Population," a conference sponsored by *The Guardian* and Third World Media Ltd. in association with the UNFPA, November 1978.

Data for singulate mean age at marriage, 1901–1971 from Dallas F. S. Fernando, "Changing Nuptuality Patterns in Sri Lanka, 1901–1971," *Population Studies* 29, no. 2 (July 1975): 179–190, Table 6, p. 185.

Data for singulate mean age at marriage, 1975, from Dallas F. S. Fernando,

"Nuptuality, Education, Infant Mortality, and Fertility in Sri Lanka," *Journal of Biosocial Science* 11 (1979): 133–140, Table 3, p. 137.

Figure 18. Adapted from van der Tak, Haub, and Murphy, "Our Population Predicament," Fig. 3, p. 9.

Figure 19. Data from United Nations, *Selected Demographic Indicators by Country 1950–2000*, pp. 12–13.

Figure 20. *Ibid.*

Figure 21. Data computed from United Nations, *World Population and Its Age-Sex Composition by Country, 1950–2000: Demographic Estimation as Assessed in 1978*, ESA/P/WP.65 (New York, 1980), pp. 2–3.

Figure 22. *Ibid.*

Figure 23. Data from United Nations, *Selected Demographic Indicators by Country 1950–2000*, pp. 12–13.

Figure 24. *Ibid.*

Figure 25. *Ibid.*

Figure 26. Data from United Nations, "Concise Report on the World Population Situation in 1970–1975 and Its Long-Range Implications," *Population Studies, No. 56*, ST/ESA/SER.A/56 (New York, 1974), Table 23, p. 59.

Figure 27. Data from 1750–1900 from Durand, "The Modern Expansion of World Population," Table 1, p. 137.

Data for 1950–2000 from United Nations, *Selected Demographic Indicators by Country 1950–2000*, p. 11.

Data for 2000–2200 from United Nations, *Long-Range Projections of World Population by Regions*, Population Division Working Paper (in preparation).

Figure 28. *Ibid.*

Figure 29. Curve of population size sketched from combination of Figure 10, this volume, and projection of plateau of population size by year 2125 between 8.0 and 14.2 billion (medium variant, 10.5 billion) found in United Nations, *Long-Range Projections of World Population by Regions*.

Curve of growth rates 8000 B.C.–present based on data in United Nations, "The Determinants and Consequences of Population Trends," Table II.1, p. 10. Future values sketched to coincide with population size. This curve is also based on that found in Ronald Freedman and Bernard Berelson, "The Human Population," *Scientific American* 231, no. 3 (September 1974): 31–39, pp. 35–37.

PART III

Figure 30. Adapted from Jonas Salk, *The Survival of the Wisest* (New York: Harper & Row, 1973), Fig. 9, p. 17. (Copyright © 1973 by Jonas Salk. Reprinted by permission of Harper & Row, Publishers, Inc.)

Figure 31. *Ibid.*, Fig. 10, p. 18.

Figure 32. *Ibid.*, Fig. 11, p. 21.

Figure 34. For a discussion of the relationship between quantity of children and quality of children see Theodore W. Schultz, "The Economics of Being Poor," *Journal of Political Economy* 88, no. 4 (August 1980): 56–79.

Figure 40. Adapted from Salk, *The Survival of the Wisest*, Fig. 21, p. 108. (Copyright © 1973 by Jonas Salk. Reprinted by permission of Harper & Row, Publishers, Inc.)

PART IV

Figure 45. Adapted from Salk, *The Survival of the Wisest*, Fig. 12, p. 23.

Figure 46. *Ibid.*, Fig. 18, p. 80.

PART V

Figure 49. Adapted from van der Tak, Haub, and Murphy, "Our Population Predicament," *Population Bulletin* 34, no. 5 (December 1979), Fig. 1, p. 2. (By permission.)

Figure 50. Sketched from combination of the previous figure with projection of plateau of population size by the year 2125 between 8.0 and 14.2 billion (medium variant, 10.5 billion) found in United Nations, *Long-Range Projections of World Population by Regions*.

Figure 51. 8000 B.C.–present based on data in United Nations, "The Determinants and Consequences of Population Trends," Table II.1, p. 10.

Future values sketched to coincide with previous figure.

This graph is also based on that found in Ronald Freedman and Bernard Berelson, "The Human Population," *Scientific American* 231, no. 3 (September 1974): 31–39, pp. 36–37.

Figure 52. Combination of preceding figures.

Related Reading

POPULATION BIOLOGY

Emlen, J. Merritt. *Ecology: An Evolutionary Approach*. Reading, Massachusetts: Addison-Wesley, 1973.

Wilson, Edward O. *Sociobiology: The New Synthesis*. Cambridge, Massachusetts: Harvard University Press, 1975.

Wilson, Edward O., and William H. Bossert. *A Primer of Population Biology*. Stamford, Connecticut: Sinauer Associates, 1971.

HUMAN POPULATION

Dumond, Dom E. "The Limitation of Human Population: A Natural History." *Science* 187 (February 28, 1975): 713–721.

Durand, John D. "The Modern Expansion of World Population." *Proceedings of the American Philosophical Society* 111 (1967): 136–159.

"The Human Population." Complete issue of *Scientific American* 231 (September 1974).

Kendall, Sir Maurice. "The World Fertility Survey: Current Status and Findings," *Population Reports*, Series M, no. 3 (July 1979).

MacDonald, Dick, ed. *The Population Story: From Now to 2000*. London, Ontario: Western Journalism Library, 1979.

Mamdani, Mahmood. *The Myth of Population Control: Family, Caste, and Class in an Indian Village*. New York: Monthly Review Press, 1972.

United Nations, Department of International Economic and Social Affairs. *World Population Trends and Prospects by Country, 1950–2000: Summary Report of the 1978 Assessment*. (ST/ESA/SER.R/33). New York, 1979.

van der Tak, Jean, Carl Haub, and Elaine Murphy. "Our Population Predicament: A New Look." *Population Bulletin* 34, no. 5 (December 1979).

Wrigley, E. A. *Population and History*. New York: World University Library, 1969.

HUMAN BIOLOGY AND HUMAN LIFE

Leakey, Richard E., and Roger Lewin. *Origins: What New Discoveries Reveal About the Emergence of Our Species and Its Possible Future.* New York: Dutton, 1977.

Salk, Jonas E. *The Survival of the Wisest.* New York: Harper & Row, 1973.

Schultz, Theodore W. "The Economics of Being Poor," *Journal of Political Economy* 88, no. 4 (August 1980): 56–79.

Stent, Gunther S. *Paradoxes of Progress.* San Francisco: W. H. Freeman and Company, 1978.

Wilson, Edward O. *On Human Nature.* Cambridge, Massachusetts: Harvard University Press, 1978.